SELF-DISCIPLINE FOR BEGINNERS

2 Books in 1: Manage Your Anger, Overcome Procrastination, Improve Your Social Skills, Create Self-Discipline and Achieve Success in Your Life

Lara Bennett

© Copyright 2020 by Lara Bennett. All rights reserved.

The material contained herein is presented with the intent of furnishing pertinent and relevant information and knowledge on the topic with the sole purpose of providing entertainment. The author should thus not be considered an expert on the topic in this material despite any claims to such expertise, first-hand knowledge, and any other reasonable claim to specific knowledge on the material contained herein. The information presented in this work has been researched to ensure its reasonable accuracy and validity. Nevertheless, it is advisable to consult with a duly licensed professional in the area pertaining to this topic, or any other covered in this book, in order to ensure the quality and validity of the advice and/or techniques contained in this material.

This is a legally binding statement as deemed so by the Committee of Publishers Association and the American Bar Association in the United States. Any reproduction, transmission, copying, or otherwise duplication of the material contained in this work are in violation of current copyright legislation. No physical or digital copies of this work, both total and partial, may not be done without the Publisher's express written consent. All additional rights are reserved by the publisher of this work.

The data, facts and description of events forthwith shall be considered as accurate unless the work is deemed to be a work of fiction. In any event, the Publisher is exempt of responsibility for any use of the information contained in the present work on the part of the user. The author and Publisher may not be deemed liable, under any circumstances, for the events resulting from the observance of the advice, tips, techniques, and any other contents presented herein.

Given the informational and entertainment nature of the content presented in this work, there is no guarantee as to the quality and validity of the information. As such, the contents of this work are deemed as universal. No use of copyrighted material is used in this work. Any references to other trademarks are done so under fair use and by no means represent an endorsement of such trademarks or their holder.

TABLE OF CONTENTS

SELF-DISCIPLINE FOR BEGINNERS
Improve Your Social Skills, Beat Procrastination, Increase Your Self-Confidence, Maximize Your Productivity and Achieve Your Goals

Introduction 3
Chapter 1 *What Does It Mean To Be Self-Disciplined* 4
Chapter 2 *Earn Why People Aren't Self-Disciplined* 7
Chapter 3 *Get To Know Yourself* 11
Chapter 4 *Don't Wait For Good Things To Happen* 16
Chapter 5 *Face Your Past, Embrace Your Present, And Don't Disgrace Your Future* ... 19
Chapter 6 *Stop Trying To Avoid Failure* 25
Chapter 7 *Set Goals And Dream Big* 31
Chapter 8 *Convert Negativity Into Positivity* 34
Chapter 9 *Remind Yourself Of Your Worth* 37
Chapter 10 *Don't Blame Others And Maintain Good Relationships* 40
Chapter 11 *Remember That Success Isn't Stagnant* 43
Chapter 12 *Don't Say You'll Try, Say You'll Do* 48
Chapter 13 *Sleep, Exercise, And Food* 50
Chapter 14 *If You Hate It, Change It* 54
Chapter 15 *Be Open To New Things* 57
Chapter 16 *Accept Criticism* 60
Chapter 17 *The World Isn't Ending* 62
Chapter 18 *Learn To Embrace Your Unconscious Mind* 64
Chapter 19 *Make The Choice To Change Your Life* 70
Conclusion 74
Description 75

MENTAL TOUGHNESS
Master Your Emotions, Develop Brain Strength With Cognitive Training Secrets, Control Your Thoughts and Feelings, Achieve the Self-Discipline to Succeed in Life

Introduction 79
Chapter 1 *Control Your Emotions* 81
Chapter 2 *Emotional Intelligence* 92
Chapter 3 *Benefits Of Being Mentally Tough* 99
Chapter 4 *Action Steps To Become Mentally Tough* 106
Chapter 5 *Practicing Mental Toughness At Your Own Pace* 127
Chapter 6 *Becoming An Alpha* 131
Chapter 7 *Being Mentally Tough In The Real World* 141
Conclusion 146
Description 148

SELF-DISCIPLINE FOR BEGINNERS

Improve Your Social Skills, Beat Procrastination, Increase Your Self-Confidence, Maximize Your Productivity and Achieve Your Goals

Lara Bennett

© Copyright 2020 by Lara Bennett
All rights reserved.
The material contained herein is presented with the intent of furnishing pertinent and relevant information and knowledge on the topic with the sole purpose of providing entertainment. The author should thus not be considered an expert on the topic in this material despite any claims to such expertise, first-hand knowledge, and any other reasonable claim to specific knowledge on the material contained herein. The information presented in this work has been researched to ensure its reasonable accuracy and validity. Nevertheless, it is advisable to consult with a duly licensed professional in the area pertaining to this topic, or any other covered in this book, in order to ensure the quality and validity of the advice and/or techniques contained in this material.
This is a legally binding statement as deemed so by the Committee of Publishers Association and the American Bar Association in the United States. Any reproduction, transmission, copying, or otherwise duplication of the material contained in this work are in violation of current copyright legislation. No physical or digital copies of this work, both total and partial, may not be done without the Publisher's express written consent. All additional rights are reserved by the publisher of this work.
The data, facts and description of events forthwith shall be considered as accurate unless the work is deemed to be a work of fiction. In any event, the Publisher is exempt of responsibility for any use of the information contained in the present work on the part of the user. The author and Publisher may not be deemed liable, under any circumstances, for the events resulting from the observance of the advice, tips, techniques, and any other contents presented herein.
Given the informational and entertainment nature of the content presented in this work, there is no guarantee as to the quality and validity of the information. As such, the contents of this work are deemed as universal. No use of copyrighted material is used in this work. Any references to other trademarks are done so under fair use and by no means represent an endorsement of such trademarks or their holder.

INTRODUCTION

Congratulations on purchasing *Self-Discipline for Beginners,* and thank you for doing so. By purchasing this book, you have put yourself well on your way to improving your life and accomplishing feats that you have only dreamed about.

The following chapters will discuss what self-discipline is, why people aren't self-disciplined, and how to become self-disciplined. Using eighteen straightforward steps, you can transform your life and get what you want to get done. So many people live in stagnancy and never accomplish what they want to accomplish simply because they don't know how to be self-disciplined. They do the same old, safe things that never get them anywhere. Part of being self-disciplined is knowing your limits, but it is also learning to expand your comfort zone and try new things.

You need some self-discipline to accomplish goals, but creating that self-discipline doesn't have to be a battle of wills between you and yourself. On the contrary, you need to learn to work with who you are rather than trying to fight that person. You are your own greatest tool, and when you can channel your skills, you will soar and reach new heights that otherwise felt impossible. You're only limited by yourself, so kick all your doubts aside and do what you need to do to be better.

There are plenty of books on this subject on the market, thanks again for choosing this one! Every effort was made to ensure it is full of as much useful information as possible, please enjoy!

CHAPTER 1
What Does It Mean To Be Self-Disciplined

What Is Self-Discipline

Self-discipline influences every part of your life, even if you are not aware of how important it is. In short, self-discipline is the skill to be autonomous over your own actions and drive yourself to accomplish your desired results. It requires you to be your own motivator. It also requires you to ensure that you don't become derailed and stay focused on the task at hand. Self-discipline is being able to get out of bed to work on a project when you'd like to nestle in your sheets for another hour. It's also knowing when you need to rest for your health versus merely wanting to for the sake of laziness. It is being able to train yourself to act in self-constructive ways rather than self-defeating ways. Ultimately, it is taking charge of your life and allowing your aspirations to become a reality through hard work and other self-driven factors.

What Self-Discipline Is Not

Many people confuse what self-discipline is with what it is not. They think that self-discipline means things that it does not. Their erroneous outlook on what it means to have self-control leads to failure and makes them feel like there's no way that they can ever have self-discipline. They become discouraged and stop trying to work on having self-discipline. Thus, you need to know what self is not so that you don't give up on having it before you've applied it properly to your life.

It is not your ability to follow diets. One of the most common areas that people focus on when it comes to self-discipline is weight loss. Let me start by saying that, yes, self-discipline can help you lose weight, but if you cannot follow certain diets, that doesn't mean that you lack self-discipline. Some diets are so restrictive and *unhealthy* that no matter how much self-control you have, you cannot follow them because your body will fight you. After all, when you heavily restrict your diet and deprive yourself severely, your body feels like its survival is being threatened, so it resists your weight loss measures. You can lose weight by using the self-discipline taught in this book to choose well-balanced meals, but no amount of self-discipline will help you accomplish fad diets.

It is not being able to take on impossible tasks. Just like the techniques in this diet cannot help you continue a fad diet (because these diets are not meant to work in the long term), it's not going to help you do things that you simply aren't capable of understanding. To make the point blatantly obvious, I'm going to use a bit of a silly example. You're not going to be able to grow wings and fly no matter how much self-discipline you have. Some goals just aren't feasible, and when you can't accomplish those goals, that failure does not reflect upon how much self-control you have.

It is not luck. It isn't something that only the fortunate have. No matter who you are, what you believe, where you come from, what you look like, you can learn to be self-disciplined. It's not a matter of fate or the odds being in your favor. It's something that you create and something that you have to maintain throughout your life. Do not neglect self-discipline from this day forward because it is absolutely in your control.

It is not just for serious people. You don't have to be a stoic person to have self-discipline. You can be a comedian. You can be laid-back. You can be emotional. Whatever you feel, whatever your personality, you can be self-disciplined because self-discipline is all about deciding when to take it easy and when to throw yourself into something entirely. It should allow you to be less serious. When you are self-disciplined, you can take time off and know when it's time to get back on track.

It is not something that you are born with or born without. While some people are more prone to impulse than others, self-discipline is something that you can nurture and practice so that you have it. Some people don't have to work to be self-disciplined, while others need to choose to be self-disciplined more consciously. In any case, it is something that is within you that you can develop whenever you want to. It takes work, but it's well worth the effort, so dedicate yourself to giving that effort rather than blaming your genes for your lack of self-discipline.

Self-discipline is not many things. It's not something that only the disciplined elite have. It's not something that you have to be born with. It doesn't mean that you'll never have the chance to be laid-back. Self-discipline allows you more flexibility and more control over your life. That's what makes it so special, and that's how it can transform your life.

Why You Need to Be Self-Disciplined

Think about all the things you've missed out on because of your self-discipline. In research by Wilhelm Hoffman in 2013, it was proven that disciplined people are overall happier. They have better focus too, which allows them to accomplish tasks that undisciplined people cannot. Self-control is vital for anyone who wants to live their life to the fullest, and without it, you may find yourself aimlessly wandering while never getting to the destination that you want. When you aren't self-disciplined, you lose chances to do the acts that will bring you the most fulfillment. You deprive your present and your future, and you get caught up in the past. To move forward, you need to be self-disciplined.

You've probably been unable to maintain stasis in your life. Your life may be filled with change, but not the good kind. Change can be helpful, but when that change causes chaos that you can't control, that's when you know that you probably aren't practicing self-discipline. You feel as though you can't control yourself, and it almost feels as though there is a monster in your body, making all the decisions. Of course, those decisions are just being made by your unconscious brain and its demands (more on that later), but it makes you feel powerless, and doing basic things soon starts to feel impossible.

It's hard for you to take charge because you can't get yourself to listen to reason. Everything that you try to build slips away, and it feels as though none of the things that you want are in your grasp. Your life is spiraling, and the more you try to stop the spiral, the less you feel like you're in control. This feeling is all too common among people who have lost or never built their self-discipline. They go from having so much promise to being completely unmotivated.

Surely, you've missed out on opportunities all because you couldn't force yourself to take up the chances that fell into your lap. This feeling of missing out should drive you to make some serious changes. Many people who aren't self-disciplined learn to lose faith in their skills and become more insecure. While insecurity can cause a lack of self-discipline, at the same time, it is fueled by a lack of self-discipline. You need to stop letting your lack of self-discipline make you feel bad about yourself and make the decision right now that you are going to do better from this moment forward. The following chapters will give you eighteen ways to start learning self-control and using it in your life. You don't have to waste your potential.

CHAPTER 2
Earn Why People Aren't Self-Disciplined

If you want to be self-disciplined, you need to first learn why people aren't self-disciplined. Several common reasons lead to people being undisciplined, and these reasons all cause projects and goals to become impossible to reach. Many of them work together to incapacitate you and prevent you from reaching your goals. You end up in the same place you started (or worse off) when you could've gotten ahead. There's no reason to let your life continue to deteriorate as you never accomplish the things that you'd like to accomplish. Let yourself be happier by embracing your need for self-discipline and acknowledging how you've failed to be self-disciplined. The more self-awareness you have, the greater chance you will have at teaching yourself self-discipline because it is something that you can learn and practice.

You Try to Take on Too Much

Most people want instant results, so they bite off more than they can chew. They Set their bars so high that even a supernatural being wouldn't have the power to accomplish that goal. It's easy to have lofty aspirations and then want for that aspiration to come instantly true, but when you take on too much at once, you're going to make it impossible to stick to what you want to accomplish. You'll end up procrastinating on the task, and then, you'll end up even more overwhelmed when you have less time to use to do quality work. There's no winning when you take on too much. If you find yourself feeling constantly overwhelmed, you're probably taking on too much. Try to slow down before you assign yourself tasks and be sure that the task that you take are ones that you can follow through on. If you can't follow through on them, rearrange your expectations. There's no sense in pushing yourself to the point of madness to get some crazy feat done. Use your past experiences to guide your current expectations of yourself so that you have room to breathe while completing whatever task you plan on completing. The more you become aware of your tendencies, the better you can be at knowing what is too much. It's okay that there's only so much that you can do before you start to get frantic.
Don't do too much at once because it will only cause you to quit what you are doing. It's all too common for people, especially people who are taking on certain projects for the first time, to get in over their heads. Know what your project will require of you and leave some buffer room in your plans so that you have room to make mistakes. When you treat a situation this way, you will be more motivated to work more efficiently without the necessity of having to work efficiently bogging you down. Take each task one step at a time, and you'll be well on your way to

completing even more tasks in the future. You don't need to do everything at once to eventually accomplish a lot.

You're Scared

One of the top reasons people act the way that they do is fear. Fear drives your unconscious brain into backing down from things that feel like a threat. Even if they aren't a threat, your brain may send a rush of chemicals through you that makes your brain and body by association, think that you are being threatened. Thus, you will react as if you are in danger rather than being able to use rational thinking to work your way through your problems. The more you avoid facing your fears, the harder it will be for you to think in ways that facilitate control. You will become bound to your impulses. When you fear something about your job, you bring that fear home, and you may start fearing certain things in your personal life as well. Thus, there's no limit to how far out of control fear can send you.

Your fears can infiltrate all parts of your life. When you are afraid about one thing, and you don't face that fear, you slowly start to become afraid of more than just that thing. You become hyper aware of the danger around you, and you feel like danger is always lurking just around the corner. You stop thinking through your issues and instead let the what-ifs rule your decisions.

The more you fear, the less control that you have. When you let fear dominate your life, you lose sight of the things that drive you to success. You become paralyzed by worries about what might happen, which never helps you be self-disciplined. You need to stop fearing so much if you ever want to become self-disciplined. Fear not, you will learn plenty of methods to accomplish this task, so you don't live a fear-driven life anymore. Be fear free so that you can regain control of your actions and your feelings.

You Don't Know What You Want

People commonly are indecisive and don't commit to anything. They flounder through life, and they hope that someday good things will come to them. Unfortunately, good things often don't just happen. Usually, you have to work for them and work to make things happen in your favor. When you don't commit to anything, you have nothing to strive for, which will lead to you remaining undisciplined. To get anywhere in life, you need to know what you want because no one else can decide that for you. Your wants can change over time, but you always must have a list of things that keep you going. When you accomplish something you want, you have to find other things to replace those completed things.

Goals keep people going, and they give them a reason to go the extra mile. Thus, when you have goals, you become self-motivated, which is a major part of being self-disciplined. When you don't have plans about what you want, you don't get that advantage. You don't have anything to get up an extra hour early for! Thus, you have to know what you want and decide what you want to work for if you want to be self-disciplined.

You're Lacking Self-Esteem

When you lack self-esteem, not much in your life is going to go well. You need some confidence to have the motivation you need to get things done. Self-esteem is how a person quantifies or qualifies their own worth as a human being. It is how you analyze your own existence and determine how much you deserve. Thus, your self-esteem greatly impacts your behavior. Self-esteem can be influenced by several factors such as upbringing, images in the media, external expectations, past or present abuse, and physical or mental illnesses.

People with low self-esteem often don't think that they deserve good things, either consciously or subconsciously. This is false, of course. All of you don't have to earn good things. You deserve to have dignity, respect, and compassion from your fellow humans, even if you have some flaws. Everyone has flaws, so you are not alone in that!

As a crucial part of your actions, your self-esteem is something that you need to tend to. If you have low self-esteem, find things to value about yourself and focus on those so that you can gradually build your self-esteem. Stop looking in the mirror and criticizing fundamental parts of yourself. Work to be a better person rather than just scrutinizing yourself to the point that you feel like you have no worth. If your self-esteem issues stem from mental health issues or past trauma, address that trauma to create a healthy mindset.

You Do Not Have a Healthy Mindset

Sometimes, people's brains aren't working as they would want them to, which makes it hard to be disciplined with yourself. People who don't have a healthy mindset or a negative outlook on life are bound to be self-defeating. They back away from opportunities because they feel so down in the dumps or otherwise uneasy. Anxiety can often limit more than help you. Thus, people whose brains look at the world through a maladaptive lens find themselves having little self-discipline and autonomy. When bad things happen, they aren't because of fate. Some are because of chance. Some are because of bad decisions, but when bad things happen, it isn't because the universe hates you. While there are so many things that you will never be able to control, you can learn to control the negative feelings you have and use them for good, and you can fight any mental dysfunction that you have.

Mental illness or negative feelings, such as grief, can make it hard to feel motivated. If you are depressed, anxious, or have other mental disorders, you may find yourself falling behind every time that you try to get ahead. This response is normal for those with mental health issues, but it doesn't have to be permanent. There are ways that you can try to motivate yourself and reduce your mental illness symptoms.

You need to tend to your mental health as well as you can to ensure that you have self-discipline. If you are ignoring any mental health struggles, you will never have the drive you need to accomplish your goals. You will be stuck feeling bad with no outlet for positive change, and your symptoms will only increase the more you neglect your problems. If you need to seek professional help or find someone who will listen to your feelings. Even the act of journaling can help you reclaim your life and your happiness. Whatever you need to do, do it so that you feel better about your mental state.

CHAPTER 3
Get To Know Yourself

Know Who You Are Up Against

If you want to get anywhere in life, you need to know who you are up against, and the most important person to know is yourself. If you don't even know yourself, you can't expect to have the self-awareness required to be self-disciplined. If you're giving yourself mixed signals, you'll naturally have mixed results, so you must be clear with yourself about who you are and what you want. Thus, take this time to learn about yourself and discover things about yourself that you have never paid attention to before. The more discovery that you do, the better you will know yourself.

You can be your own worst enemy. People often torture themselves with their expectations. I've encountered far too many people who held themselves at impossible standards or tried to be someone who they weren't. In all cases, these people failed to ever get what they wanted. They floundered through life, and sometimes, they had limited success, but this success was usually limited to just one sphere of their life. So, while they may have had professional success, they lacked self-discipline in their personal lives. When you start to know yourself, you open yourself up to success in all areas of your life. Try being your friend rather than working against yourself.

You can also learn to be your own best friend. Start being the person who is your number one supporter. It's great to have people in your life who are willing to support you, but you need to support yourself just as much. Get to know who you are as well as you know your best friend because you deserve that level of self-awareness. Teach yourself to embrace the qualities that make you unique because those are the qualities that we most often love about our best friends, and they are the qualities that most make you who you are.

What you think you are defines your behaviors. If you think you're a bad person, you're going to become a bad person. That's just how your brain works. It takes the messages that you hear most, and it marks those messages as the most truthful, even if they are not. Thus, when you repeat certain thoughts, you have the power to change your brain's default settings. How cool is that? You have the power to shift how your entire brain processes and how it applies the information, and all you have to do is redefine yourself.

When you become predictable, you can challenge bad behaviors and maintain good ones. The point is not to become boring or lose all spontaneity. Rather, it is to learn your common behaviors so that you can act in ways that better reflect and support who you are at your core. The first step to change is awareness, so become of the things that you're habitually doing wrong and address those. Encourage yourself to continue the habits that help you reach your goals and become more self-disciplined. What these habits look like will vary by person, but with a little digging into yourself, you can easily find them.

You'll feel lost if you have no idea who you are. When put like that, it seems so obvious. You're going to feel lost if you're plucked from your home and plopped into a forest with no map. Make a mental map of your personality. Know where you came from, where you are, and where you'd like to go to make your life a million times easier. When you get to know yourself, you add direction to your life, and without that direction, you don't have the motivation or understanding that you need to act with discipline.

If you don't have a firm idea about what you stand for, you'll never have the self-identity that you need for self-discipline. So, knowing yourself is about more than knowing what your hair color is or how you feel during any given moment. It's about knowing what you believe in. Everyone has things in their life that they would risk it all for. You have to know what those things are and let them be a part of the rest of your life because those passions are what encourage you to keep going even when things get hard.

The bottom line is that you need to know yourself to have any self-control. Your brain thrives on patterns and habits that it can understand, so by knowing those patterns, you can master yourself and be in charge of your actions. When you don't know who you are, you spin a circle waiting for the day when you can do something different. You become restless because you know that you want something, but for the life of you, you can't figure out what that something is. Stop being ignorant about yourself, and start going on the wonderful adventure that is self-discovery.

How to Get to Know Yourself

While it's probably pretty clear why you need to know who you are, you may be wondering how to accomplish that goal. If you're one of those people who has been disconnected from yourself for *years*, it may feel overwhelming to consider that maybe you're not the person who you think that you are. You may have been hiding behind a façade for years without really knowing it. You have gotten so obsessed with career success that you've forgotten the things that make you feel alive, or you've stopped connecting as deeply with the people around you. When you push away your true self, any part of it, you become drained and less able to resist temptation. You're vulnerable when you deny a part of your identity.

Keep a journal. Keeping a journal is one of the best practices that you can have in general, but it is particularly good for self-discovery. Journaling not only is a great way to help you track patterns about yourself and become more aware of your emotions, but it will also make you physically healthier. Research shows that just fifteen minutes a day of journaling can help lower your blood pressure because it reduces stress. Those who journal may get sick less and have a decreased risk of heart disease. It's a lot easier to focus on self-discovery when you're feeling good than when you're feeling bad. Plus, when you write things down, you are more likely to mind them in the future, a technique that you'll also use when it comes to goal setting.

Visualize who you would like to be. A visualization is a tool used by celebrities such as Oprah to help them manifest success. When you visualize, you create a self in your head that you want to bring to life, and by visualizing, your brain is more likely to remember what you want and help you act accordingly. To visualize, all you have to do is imagine the person you want to be. Let's say that you want to be a parent, married to a nice spouse, and living in a nice house. Close your eyes, and imagine yourself in your dream house. Think in detail about what this dream house would look like. Now, imagine your spouse. Think about what they would look like, sound like, smell like, etc. Imagine how all your senses would be engaged in this dream future, and imagine how you'd react to all the stimuli. Finally, imagine your child. Imagine holding that child and think of how you would feel and all the things that you would like to teach your kid. Visualization is as simple as that. Of course, what you want will probably look incredibly different, but nevertheless, you can imagine it just as vividly.

Experiment with hobbies and new endeavors you've always wanted to try. Try to get back in touch with what you enjoy doing. There's no time to waste in life, so you might as well be doing things that make you happy instead of doing things that cause you to drag your feet. Many people suppress hobbies and activities that they like for the sake of practicality. They think there's no way to fit those interests into their lives, but that is false. You can fit enjoyment into your schedule because by doing things that you enjoy, you awaken parts of yourself that you've been neglecting.

Determine your strengths. Know what you're good at, and use that as a starting point for everything that you do. Play up your strengths because when you play up your strengths, you can accomplish tasks with more ease and confidence. This step may seem obvious, but many people don't realize what their strengths are. They fool themselves into thinking that they are good at certain things while being unaware of their true strengths. You have to accept the strengths you have, even if they are not the strengths that you would prefer. You can build new strengths with time and discipline, but until then, focus on what you can do instead of what you can't.

Determine your weaknesses. Just as much as you need to know what you're good at, you also need to know what you're bad at. Again, be honest with yourself. Don't lie to yourself about your weaknesses because that will get your nowhere. If you have a bad temper, fess up to that bad temper rather than denying that it exists. Denial doesn't make you happy. It makes you feel pent up and out of control. When you know your weaknesses, you can work on ameliorating them. As you embrace your weaknesses, you'll start to see that knowing your weaknesses can be just as powerful as knowing your strengths.

Identify your core values. Know the core belief system that drives your decision making. If you believe in equality, act accordingly. Treat people with equality and don't make exceptions. Of course, values can be flexible, but there are certain beliefs that you cannot act against without being a hypocrite, and those are the ones that you need to integrate into every part of your life. These values shouldn't differ because you're at work or because you're at home. When you act with hypocrisy, you compromise yourself because hypocrisy is the same in spirit as repressing yourself.

Analyze why you do what you do. You need to know why you do your negative habits and why you do your good habits to understand who you are. Don't just acknowledge these habits, but also break them down. What causes you to do them? Boredom? Past trauma? Because you've always done it that way? Ask yourself why you continue to repeat certain things because you might find that you don't have a good reason, and when that's the case, it might be time for a shift in your behavior. Change isn't easy, but when you use an analytical lens, you will be inspired to do it.

Challenge what you think you know about yourself. You're not who you were ten years ago. Repeat after me, "I'm not who I was ten years ago or even a year ago." People are dynamic, and if you're holding onto who you think you should be or who you used to be, you're doing yourself a grave disservice. It's okay to evolve. That's what you should be doing, and if you're not, you have some serious issues that you need to address. Don't put yourself into a box. People will expect certain things of you based on what you've done before, but you don't have to meet those expectations if that doesn't feel genuine anymore. It's okay to say, "That was once me, but it's not anymore."

Observe and question how other people see you. Knowing what other people think about you can help you know yourself. Do not let other people define you, but use their perspectives to see a broader view of yourself. Rely on your own instincts about who you are first and foremost, but if you're in denial about who you are, acknowledging how other people see you can be a wake-up call and show you how much self-discovery you have left to do. Sometimes, your loved ones do know you better than yourself, but only when you deny your own identity (which many people do to varying degrees).

Be more in tune with your emotions. Don't be afraid of your feelings. Humans often like to think that they are rational beings, but at our core, we are emotion. We work based upon some logical principles, but when our emotions are involved, we become compromised. This isn't a bad thing, but when you deny your emotions, you cannot control yourself. Why? Because emotions are a vital part of human behavior, and to pretend you aren't motivated by them would be harmful. Your emotions are your number one driver in life. They motivate you, and they allow you to know who you are because how you respond emotionally to stimuli shows much about your emotional makeup and brain's responses.

Don't stop learning about yourself even when you think you know it all. You're going to change, and you're going to grow. With that growth, you will become a person who you might not initially recognize. Your wants and the way you respond to your emotions may change, which means that when it comes to yourself, you have to continue your education. You can never stop pondering who you are and what your place in this world is. When you do stop learning about yourself, you will lose track of who you are, and you will feel so unclear about your own identity that you can't possibly have self-discipline.

CHAPTER 4
Don't Wait For Good Things To Happen

They say that good things happen to those who wait, and while there is some logic in this adage, it's not what I want you to do going forward. The point of the adage is patience, but it sends the message that if you wait long enough, the universe will change your situation for you, which isn't going to happen. Ever. You may have to wait for certain good outcomes that you want, but when you wait for good things to happen, you leave what happens to fate rather than taking charge of it yourself. You can't hope good things will happen and then do nothing about it! That's the opposite in spirit to self-discipline.

Take an active role in your life. It's your life, so if you aren't happy with it, do something about it. Waiting for good things to happen is passive. It means that you are sitting around and hoping that good things will be done to you, but that very rarely happens in life. Good things are often the product of your decisions and your actions. It's true that sometimes, after much waiting, good things will pop up seemingly out of nowhere, but you have no control over how and when that will happen. You're relying on other people and nature to give you what you want, which gives you no autonomy over what happens to you.

Stop putting things off until tomorrow. If you want to change, do it today. Procrastinating doesn't serve you in any way. Don't wait for a better time to get started because things will always pop up, and the timing will never be perfect. If you want to make a career change, start working on it now. You don't have to wait until after you've gotten your mid-year review. Waiting doesn't get your anywhere, so while I'm not saying to quit your job the minute you want a new one, I am saying that when you want to change, you can start putting steps and plans into motion to ease yourself into that change.

Define good things in new ways. You define what in your life is good, which means that you have the power to say that simple things are good things. Good things don't have to be limited to life changing happenings like winning the lottery. If you look closely, you will realize those good things can come in small packages. Good things can happen daily if you reassess what qualifies as a good thing. A good thing can be something as simple as being able to get your work done on time. While that seems like the bare minimum, sometimes just getting through a hard day is a good thing! Good things happen to those who look for good things in even the grimmest of situations.

Waiting aimlessly brings no joy. If you're sitting around unhappy, you're not living a very good life. You're not in the mindset to accomplish. You're in the mindset to mope. You'll never get happier by waiting. Some people wait for good things for *years*. People are challenged by enough waiting for water to boil! So, waiting for years to have any goodness is depleting. It drains you of the motivation to be self-disciplined. You feel like happiness is so far away that there's no point in delaying gratification. You start to believe that instant gratification is the only gratification that you'll ever get, but that doesn't have to be the case.

In the 1960s, a Stanford experimenter, Walter Mischel, conducted the famous marshmallow experiments. In these experiments, young kids were put in a room, and an adult put a marshmallow in front of them. He told them that if they waited fifteen minutes before eating the marshmallow, they could have another marshmallow. Some kids were able to delay their gratification and earn the second marshmallow, some waited a few minutes before eating the marshmallow, and some ate the marshmallow as soon as the adult left the room. As the kids grew older, further research showed that the kids who were able to wait for the second marshmallow were more successful in their endeavors for the forty years after the initial experiment that they followed. The other kids tended more to impulsivity and impulsive behaviors like drug or alcohol use. Thus, the experiment showed the power of delayed gratification, and that cannot be denied, but while you could withstand fifteen minutes of delay, waiting years is much more daunting.

Most books on self-discipline suggest that you learn to delay gratification, and there's some truth to this. Self-discipline does require you to delay gratification to some extent. You have to be able to hold off doing certain things now so that you can have better things in the future. For example, instead of buying ten cheap t-shirts, you could save up for the expensive one that you really love. Even so, you still need to find gratification daily. This gratification can come from little places, but to be happy, you have to constantly be trying to find the good that surrounds you. You have to be patient for long-term goals to come to fruition, but that doesn't mean that you can't treat yourself every now or then or find things that make you happy right now.

Learn to love the process— that's how you can find gratification daily. Love the journey more than you love the results. The results are great, but the purpose of anything should include the path you take to get what you want. If you're going on a hike, you don't want to just enjoy the beautiful view from the peak of the mountain. You also want to enjoy the wildlife around you on your trek upward. Stop every so often and take in the beauty of the process. Appreciate it in all its glory because taking steps to improve yourself is a beautiful thing.

Don't expect good chances to fall from the sky. Opportunities don't happen out of the blue. You may not expect them, but they happen because of things you've done and the things that the people and things around you have done. Mostly, they are built from good things you've decided to further your goals. Stop sitting around for a chance to change your life and make your chance. You're in control of the chances you have when you decide that you want to be.

Good things are all around you right now. Look around wherever you are sitting right now. Take in the good of it. What in your environment right now gives you joy? Focus on that thing for a few moments and embrace it. Appreciate it for all it does for you. Just because the good things may not be your long-term goal doesn't mean that they don't exist. In life, no matter how grim a situation, there are always things that can make you feel content. There is peace to be found within your basic life. You don't need to make grand dreams come true to find that peace. All you have to do is accept the goodness and use it to build more goodness.

Ultimately, you are in charge of your own destiny. There's no one else in the world who can define what happens to you. Things may not always go to plan, but you're in charge of your reactions. You decide how you frame the narratives that surround what happens to you. The power to add meaning to your life is a wonderful way that we can use our emotions to further the facts that surround us.

CHAPTER 5
Face Your Past, Embrace Your Present, And Don't Disgrace Your Future

Your past, present, and your future are three important facets of who you are, and many people neglect at least one of these parts of themselves. In the process, they are unable to stick to what they set out to do because they have not made peace with who they are now, who they were, or who they will be. You need to interact with all parts of yourself so that you can confidently stick to the plans that you make.

Face Your Past

Your past is the formative experience of who you are today. It determines how you feel, and it determines your brain's natural responses to stimuli. In your most formative years, you learned that certain actions lead to certain responses, and sometimes, these associations are positive, but they can also be negative. Everyone has negative things in their past that can make it hard to move forward. Alternatively, for some, the past may be an idealized time, and they may pine for the golden years that they wish they could have back. In either case, such a mentality can be dangerous to both your present and your future, which is why it is so important that you face your past.

Accept that your past is yours and that you cannot change it. The past is not something that you change no matter how hard you try, but you can reframe it and interpret it in new ways that better reflect who you are now. Your past belongs to you, so it can mean whatever you chose it means to your current self. It doesn't have to incapacitate you if you don't let it. It can be used as energy to drive yourself into the future. It only has as much power as you give it, so give that power wisely.

Acknowledge the trauma that you have, even if it is hard to face. You never have to forget the trauma or downplay its significance, nor should you try to do that, but you do have to learn to think about the trauma and give its existence the weight that it deserves. This idea applies to both big and little trauma. Whatever lingering trauma you have from the past, you need to learn from it and to accept that it has happened to you and that there's nothing you can do to erase the hurt that you once felt (and maybe still do feel).

Analyze how your past has changed you. Once you have acknowledged your trauma, you can start to explore how that trauma (or the joy in your life) has changed who you are now. Think about all the things that you might've done differently if you hadn't had the trauma. Think about who you might be without it. Don't let yourself regret the path that you did take, but see how the past has made you who you are, and visualize how it can be part of the person you want to be. Your past will always influence who you are, but it is not the sole determiner. Don't keep painful reminders that make you feel worse about your present. If you have old trinkets that only make you feel bad about yourself, then it might be time to get rid of those things. For example, if you have a pair of jeans from forty pounds ago, get rid of them. It doesn't matter if you plan on losing weight. Get rid of them because they are a part of the past that makes you feel pressure to lose weight when that pressure doesn't help you. When you do lose weight with self-discipline and care for your body, you can buy new jeans that represent the present you. Those will make you feel a whole lot better than those old ones that make you feel like a failure.

Forgive but don't forget. If it helps you to forgive people who have hurt you, do so. That doesn't mean that you have to let them back in your life or that you even have to talk to them ever again. It just means that you release yourself from the hold that hurt has on you. You take the burden of your hurt off yourself and relinquish its power over you. Don't forget what happened. Blocking those memories out isn't helpful, but let yourself move past the pain and walk forward free of bitterness.

Understand that what you remember isn't always fully true. Memory is a fuzzy thing. It's common for people to misremember what happened to them. Even just a casual conversation can shift your memory of past events. Memory is malleable, so know that what you remember will never be the full story. While you can remember the broad strokes of something, the details are often misremembered. There's nothing wrong with that. Memory is influenced by your feelings and experiences. That's all, and knowing that, you can realize that the past isn't as powerful as you might think it is. It's not changeable like I said, but you can reshape it in ways that bring you peace.

Find things to be grateful for regarding your past. Even if you think your past is completely awful, there has to be at least something good in that past. Think of something good and be grateful that the good thing happened. It can be something small, but small things can be a salvation for someone who is struggling. Maybe your dad was a negligent drunk, but you remember how he used to take you for ice cream, and that was the one time that you enjoyed with him. That little memory can give you something to clutch so you can work through the harder memories.

Know that you are not your past. Whatever happened to you back then, you aren't that trauma or joy. You are yourself, and you are your present yourself. You cannot be reduced to the person you used to be just as you cannot be reduced to the person you will be five years from now. You get to be whoever you want going forward. You're not stuck being the hurt person from before. Your past is not something that you can get rid of. It may seem impossible to emerge from your past, but with time and some self-reflection (and maybe some therapy), it is possible. You don't have to keep feeling pinned down by things that once occurred. Free yourself from the past and start living in the present!

Embrace Your Present

Your present is the one thing you get to control fully, which means it is the time when you can fully embrace self-discipline. In the present, you make the decisions that honor your past while building a future that makes you excited about your life and feel as though you have a purpose. The present is the part of your life that you should mostly pay attention to because it is the part that you get to dictate, and it can be whatever you make of it. The present is where you find joy and contentment, so don't waste it. Once the present becomes the past, it is too late to do anything with it, so don't let the present pass by before you can catch it and hold it for the few moments it is here.

Stay focused on what you are doing now. When you're working on a project or enjoying time with loved ones, don't let your brain drift and start thinking about things that you're going to be doing tomorrow. When you waste time fretting when you could be doing, you set yourself up for failure. You make it harder to get anything done because your attention is fragmented. It's hard enough to focus as it is, so don't let your brain wander too far beyond here and now or else you'll get yourself into trouble. Getting in the habit of worrying about the future will make you more stressed than functional! Stress only further drags you from the present. The more stressed you get, the harder it becomes to be present, so try to manage your stress before it gets too bad. Don't let it pull you away from what you need to accomplish.

Be present with other people. One of the most important things that you can do right now is to be present with your loved ones or coworkers. It's hard to deal with people who are spacey and who are working a week ahead (mentally). You'll benefit greatly from quality time with your loved ones, and if you're worried about a work email that you have to send, then you're not going to be present, and your relationships will suffer. Leave the email off when you're at home, and don't worry about home matters while you're at work. By doing this, you'll be able to be fully present when you interact with others rather than rushing through social activities or barely paying attention.

Don't worry about things you can't control. There's so much in life that's not in your power. Most of the future is not something that you can guarantee. You don't even know if you'll be alive tomorrow, so you might as well stop fearing what could happen, and you should start taking charge of what you can control. That's the key to self-discipline— using the power you do have rather than trying to take charge of things that are impossible to take charge of. For example, you can't control when you get a raise, but you can work as hard as you're able and prove that you deserve a raise. Present actions increase your command over the future even though the future is still up in the air. You can't control who will die. You can't ensure that you won't get sick or hurt. You don't know if your boss will fire you. You know so little, but that's okay. Uncertainty allows you chances for growth. It allows you to dive into experiences that you never thought you would dive into, so take changes in stride.

Know that right now is precious. People commonly say that the present is a gift, and though it might be trite, it's true. Right now is your chance to take action. You can't act in the future, and you certainly can't act in the past, so you have to do it right now. There's no sense waiting to do whatever it is you want to do. Having self-discipline is knowing that you're going to act right now, and you're not going to let yourself become a passive bystander in your own life. The present is filled with beauty. All you have to do is find that beauty and channel it. Stop looking at the ugliness and find what you can do instead of what you can't.

Let yourself find enjoyment today instead of hating right now. There's no sense being bitter over what is happening in your life. Some things in life, like the loss of a loved one, are devastating, but that doesn't mean you have to give in to the devastation. It takes time to recover from hurt and tragedy, but you can start to take steps forward, small but important steps, any time you want. Even if you are sad, you can find small moments to enjoy life. People who are grieving often feel that they don't deserve to smile and that they need to sit with their gloom, but it's okay to laugh every once in a while. That doesn't take away from the sorrow you feel. It's just a reprieve and a slow step forward towards recovery. Don't push yourself too hard to get better too fast, but let yourself have hope that there are still good things in the world.

Being present in your present is one of the best things that you can do for yourself because it allows you to take action. If you aren't present, you have little power over what happens to you. You become just a cog in the machine, and you let life spin you around without taking an autonomous role. You are a unique person, so let your actions reflect that. Share your ideas in the meeting instead of keeping them to yourself. Do things that make you feel good. Embrace the wonderful elements of life that keep you going in the hardest times. That's self-discipline. It is being present and choosing to be present because that's what you need to do to have success.

Don't Disgrace Your Future

Your future isn't something that you can control, but it's an important part of who you are because no matter how much you try to be present, there will be times when you feel the future nagging at you. You'll be in bed, staring at the ceiling, and you won't be able to stop thinking about what the morning will bring. The thought of all the things that could happen will keep you up, and you'll have to get up and drag your feet to work feeling exhausted and shrouded in negativity. The future can make you feel awful, but it doesn't have to. Ideally, it should make you feel excited. It should be the thing that makes you want to leap from your bed and do the best job you can in all areas of your life. Once you learn not to fear it, you can see that the future can help you embrace your present. You'll learn not to let future fears make you feel hopeless. You'll learn not to disgrace your future by expecting the best from it instead of the worst. Trust me; the future isn't as scary as you think. If it was, our lives would be pretty grim.

Dream about a better future, not the nightmares that could (but probably won't) happen. Start and end each day by letting yourself visualize what your future could be. By visualizing what you want to happen each day, you set yourself up for success, and your brain will process your visualization better if you do it just before and just after you get up. Imagine yourself where you'd like to be and imagine how you'll feel when you accomplish your goals. Let this feeling carry you through your day and reassure you that you can deal with the future no matter what happens.

The future is terrifying. There's no getting around that. It's even more terrifying because of all the unknown variables that you can't plug into an equation and simply solve for x. You must live with that uncertainty, and if you learn to live with that, you can be more successful than you ever imagined. Acknowledge what scares you about the future. Don't run away from your fears because when you run away from your fears, they only magnify. By dragging your fears into the light, you can realize that they aren't so scary after all. What you fear in your worst-case scenario version of the future isn't realistic. Our brains tend to catastrophize situations, but the future isn't that bad. It will have bad moments, but if you go about it the right way, you ensure that those bad moments are less common. You can't escape unpleasantness that will come, but your life is unlikely to be as unpleasant as you think that it will be. Again, attitude matters. If you expect the worst, that's what the future will give you. The energy you put into your visions of the future will be returned to you when that future becomes the present.

Planning is a present activity that you can do to put the odds in your favor. It's something that humans often do without thinking, but intentionally planning has more power. Don't get too carried away with planning, but making basic plans can help guide your decisions and make the future less scary. Don't be rigid with your plans because that will only cause you to worry more when things don't go exactly how you predicted, but be firm with yourself on having plans. You need these plans for self-discipline. Without them, there's no point in striving to be self-disciplined because self-discipline requires a game plan and a set standard that you are going to hold yourself to. Don't be afraid to expect a lot of yourself as you plan. The worst that can happen is you miss the mark and have to try again!

Your future is sacred, so don't dismiss it. It should be something that you value, not something that you look upon with apathy. The future is exciting and anxiety-inducing, but it is well worth the wait. It gives you hope in your present, and it allows you to redeem and reclaim your past. The future is a coloring book that you get to color in. Lines will be drawn for you, but you can challenge what those lines mean based on the choices you make. You add life to your future. No one else can.

Know that what you do now will impact your future. No matter what you are doing now, it's going to change your future. Every decision that you make influences what will happen to you, so make decisions wisely. With that being said, you don't have the benefit of hindsight when you're making your decisions, so don't be too hard on yourself for decisions you made when you didn't have all the information. All you can do is make the best decisions that you can at the moment you make them. Doing more than that would require superpowers, and you're only human!

Don't villainize the future. It's not something inherently bad or ugly. It doesn't want to hurt you or make your life harder. It's something that just happens; the future doesn't have to be your foe. You can turn it into an ally. Make it a source of goodness rather than a source of sorrow. Think of all the wonderful things that are still to happen in your life. Acknowledge that bad things happen, but that those bad things don't have to prevent you from having future joy. Let the future be sacred, but don't become so obsessed with it that you can't live in the present because when all you can think about is the future, you disgrace your future. After all, the future depends on your present to shape it, so if you aren't present now, you'll have wasted time you could have used to create a better future.

CHAPTER 6
Stop Trying To Avoid Failure

The Fear of Failure

When you're afraid of failure, you cannot live your life normally. You become a nervous wreck, afraid of doing anything wrong. The fear spreads until it is devouring every part of your life. Nothing is safe from this evil fear that plagues too many people across the world. The fear of failure is something that nearly one-third of all adults in the United States face. Accordingly, it is one of the biggest fears that people have, and it can interrupt people's goal-setting and goal-reaching incredibly easily. People who are afraid of failure cannot be self-disciplined because they spend too much time thinking about what may go wrong to the point that they back away from what may go right. They become so afraid that they are paralyzed by their fear, and instead of sticking to plans, they run away as soon as the plans get hard. People figure that there's no point trying because, in the end, they are going to fail no matter how hard they work. This mentality leads to the indecisiveness and fickle nature of those who don't have self-discipline. Fear not, though, this fear of failure can be combated.

One of the worst impacts of the fear of failure is self-sabotage. People who are afraid of failure strive to stay in place. They curl up in their safe little bubbles and refuse to try new things because that feels less dangerous than going out into the world and trying. Unfortunately, this behavior does not lead to happiness. It only causes self-sabotage. People let their fears dictate their life, so every time that something good presents itself, they hide and back away from the opportunity instead of taking it. A person working on a work project that could lead to their promotion, for instance, may get so worried that they will fail that they avoid working on the project and instead fret about how it can go wrong. The person then doesn't get the promotion because their work was subpar. They became a self-fulfilling prophecy. By saying, "I can't do this because I'll fail," they really did fail, more than they would have if they gave their best effort.

When you have a fear of failure, any mistake can compromise your sense of worth. It can make you feel like the worst person in the world, and it can make you think that you don't deserve success. It convinces you that you're better off being discontent but safe. The fear of failure lies to you, as all fears do, but you can't listen to it because it will slowly kill you if you do. You don't feel like yourself when you prohibit yourself from attempting the feats that will make you feel the most alive.

People with a fear of failure are unable to do much of anything because they push away the tools that will lead to success. Those with the fear of failure will fail because they will refuse to do things that will lead them to their goals. They will resist opportunities in favor of existing in their safe bubbles of false security. They will suffer in their stagnancy, not understanding that they can emerge from their bubbles and fight the insecurities that are brewing in their bellies. Don't be a person consumed by failure. Rise above these fears, and you'll see that your fear is overblown. The only true failure is failing to try.

Why Failure Is Good

It may seem like failure is always bad, but that's not the case. Failure is one of the most beneficial experiences that you will ever face. It won't feel good. In the moment of your failure, it will never feel like a win, but it doesn't have to debilitate you. One failure doesn't have to stop you from ever trying again. Self-disciplined people can push forward even when they make mistakes. Self-disciplined people know that eating a piece of candy forbidden by your diet doesn't mean throwing away the whole diet. Self-disciplined people are not perfect. They are not robots. Being self-disciplined doesn't mean you never do the wrong thing. It doesn't mean that you never stray from the plan. It simply means that when you do wander from your intentions that you're able to get back on task and reorient yourself amidst the changes that you face.

Failures help you learn how to do better next time. They show you that you can expect more of yourself and that you should. They teach you that you've got to keep going to get what you want. You shouldn't look at failure as something that discourages you from your goal. It should be a reminder that your goal is out there, but you just have to adapt the path you use to get there. Things didn't go as planned. So what? It's not a big deal. Brush yourself off and keep going because unless your interests have changed, there's no reason to back down from what you want until you don't want it anymore.

Further, failures can help you learn about yourself. Sometimes, you realize that you didn't want what you thought you wanted until failure shows you what really brings you joy. Maybe you thought you wanted to complete an assignment at work, but when you start on the project, you realize that your overarching want was to get closer to a coworker who you admire. When the project goes south, you might realize that the project itself wasn't what was driving you. Rather, it was the desire to be closer to another person. Sometimes, you don't know what you want until you try. Lots of kids go to college with one major, enroll in a few classes, and realize that the major they thought they wanted was completely different from the one they chose. Mistakes can help show you what you really want and put you back on course to achieving your dreams.

Motivation is also a byproduct of failure. When you fail, and you don't let that failure consume you, your failure can make you feel even more devoted to your cause. You'll have the urge to prove your doubters wrong and show that you accomplish whatever you set your mind to. Failure can give you an extra jolt of energy and help you focus your mind back on what you want. Many great people have used failure to help them keep going. Thomas Edison notably tried to make the lightbulb hundreds of times. He made a myriad of mistakes, but because of his tenacity, he came out ahead. He used each mistake as a chance to do better.

Failure teaches you to handle disappointment, which is a crucial part of success. Successful people are used to being disappointed. They know that life sometimes has a way of throwing curveballs. Failure shows you how to handle the unpredictability of life. It encourages you to keep going even when things don't go your way. Those who have had a lot of failures know how to respond to disappointment while those who haven't let themselves fail don't have as much experience. While disappointment will never feel good, failure shows you how to not let your misguided expectations destroy your ambition. Self-disciplined people know how to accept disappointment and not let it ruin other opportunities.

Additionally, failure lets you be open to new opportunities. When you fail, there are a million chances to do better. If you mess up, you may discover other avenues you want to explore. You get to explore and figure out where to go next. It's remarkable to be able to take the bad elements from an old experience and use them to create a whole new experience. You can't fail forever. Eventually, you'll find a chance that fits your needs and has the results you want. Failure only leads you closer to success because, contrary to popular belief, it doesn't steer you away from your goals.

Humans are bound to fail from time to time, so failure makes you human. Maybe you'd rather be a superhero or an animal, but because you are not, you'll have to accept that humanity is part of you. You're not wired to be perfect. You're wired to operate as best as you can, and in times of tumult, that is going to have to be enough. When you fail, you are connected to every other human on this earth. You share the bond of being pushed down and trying to get back up. That's what humans have been doing for our entire history. We have evolved, but we still have to struggle to survive and thrive.

Because failure thrives on low self-esteem, failure forces you to confront your insecurities. When you fail, you may start to get that insecure feeling in your stomach. You feel like something is wrong with you, and you think that if you were someone else that you would have been able to succeed. Insecurity does not reflect the truth. It reflects your fears, and it tries to convince you that you'll only ever fail, but upon feeling that insecurity, instead of listening to it, you can challenge it. You can bring it to your consciousness and figure out why the situation makes you feel so insecure. Once you know why that insecurity exists, you can fight that feeling each time you get it until you feel secure.

Flexibility is another lesson that can be taught by failure. When you fail, you learn that you cannot be rigid. If you're attempting something, there will be bumps in the road, and sometimes, you'll be able to drive over them, but other times, you'll have to take a detour. When you're flexible and allow these changes, you teach yourself that you can get through anything. You can endure whatever life throws your way because your self-discipline keeps you going. Flexibility ensures that you don't get so caught up in your old plan that you lose track of the opportunities that failure can bring.

Failure can be an immense help to you if you let it be. You don't have to hate yourself for failing. You don't have to throw in that towel. You don't have to let the failure destroy you. Those are not the behaviors of self-disciplined people. Self-disciplined people know that the moments after the failure are the ones that you most need to push through. It is in those moments that you show your true character and determine whether you are the kind to accomplish goals or the kind to merely imagine goals. Let failure be a good influence in your life rather than a bad one.

How to Accept Failure

There are some steps that you can take to start accepting the failure in your life. These tasks are straightforward, but for people who are terrified of failure, these tasks will be a challenge. It may take weeks or even months for you to start feeling less afraid of failure. Changes will not happen overnight, but you will start to feel a change in your mind as you remind yourself of your need to accept the failure in your life. You may not accept it now, but if you keep telling yourself that you do, you someday will.

Know that your failures don't impact your worth. You aren't a lesser person because of your failures. Let's say that you yelled at your husband for something you later realize that he didn't do, or you yell at your kid for not putting her shoes away when you were actually mad at your wife. These mistakes don't mean you're a bad person. Things happen. It doesn't mean you should continue to let that same mistake happen because if you don't learn from your mistakes, what is the point? It does mean that when you turn in an assignment late or miss lunch with your mom that you're not a worse person than you were before those things. You don't deserve suffering because of your well-intentioned failures. You still deserve love and respect. By keeping this in mind, you will be able to respond to failure by doing better next time instead of shutting down and refusing to take anything constructive from your failure.

Realize that avoiding potential failure will only make you fail to do anything. Success requires failure, so if you don't let yourself fail, you won't let yourself succeed either. You can't keep avoiding failure because when you do that, you end up unhappy. You don't have to dive into projects that you know are doomed to fail, but you do need to push your boundaries because sticking to things you know you'll succeed at (even if they are challenging) is not living your life to the fullest. You deserve to take advantage of every chance this world has to offer and to use those chances to improve yourself. No matter who you are, you have so much untapped potential. You might have to be creative to find it, but it is there. Look at failures as challenges. Instead of using the word failure, try swapping the word out with the word challenge. Your mistake wasn't a failure; it was a challenge to do things differently. It was a challenge to push your boundaries further. It was a challenge to make amends. It was a challenge to work harder. There are so many health challenges that failure can provide. Don't waste those challenges. Use them to the fullest extent that you are able because a failure that is not a challenge is a wasted opportunity.

You don't need to be perfect; stop trying! Stop using black and white thinking. This kind of thinking leads to people thinking bipolar. They see things as wrong or right, black or white, day or night. In life, not everything is perfect or a failure. There are in-betweens— gray areas— and in these gray areas, you have the chance to do better and challenge your own expectations. Perfection brings you clones. It doesn't bring you innovative ideas. Things that aren't perfect are more unique because perfection isn't real. It is a standard set by the status quo of our society. For example, society has standards about what a perfect body looks like, but this perfect body doesn't necessarily function better than other bodies. It does allow people to do more than those with "unideal" bodies. This perfect body is an unobtainable societal construct. Thus, things that aren't deemed perfect still have value. You get to create the value. You get to show the world the beauty in the imperfect.

Stop putting so much pressure on yourself. Everyone likes to be successful. We're taught from a young age how gratifying success is, and too often, we're taught that success looks like one thing— money, fame, and power— but you don't have to pressure yourself to be that. Success can mean whatever you want it to mean, and that version of success is just as valid as anyone else's. Don't force yourself to be someone you are not and don't feel like you have to reach your goals quicker than other people. It's okay to take your time. It's okay if you're eight-two years old and only just now striving for a goal normally completed by eighteen-year-olds! Life isn't a race. It's an exploration, so let yourself explore and don't make that exploration feel like a chore. Take a breath, and let yourself be. As long as you are reaching for your aspirations and propelling yourself forward, you're doing great. Self-discipline is about knowing what pace is right for you.

If people mock you for your mistakes, particularly people who have no reason to dislike you, that says more about them than it does you. There are always going to be people out there who are going to discourage you from what you are doing, whether because they are jealous, bitter, insecure, or unhappy, among other reasons people are hateful. Their hate doesn't mean that your failure is irredeemable. Sometimes, when you make mistakes, it is your own fault that the other person is upset. You ruin relationships, and there's no going back, but even in those cases, while you might not be able to save the relationship that you hurt, you can still be a better person. Don't expect other people to forgive you for things you've done to them, but you should be able to forgive yourself.

The more you let yourself fail, the easier it will be to rebound from failure. I know you don't want to fail more than you need to, but the good news is that the more you fail, the easier it gets to continue. As you get used to failure and realize that it's not as scary as you thought, you will see that time is wasted when you spend it worrying about failure. That time could be spent trying something new. It could be used to better develop yourself to be resilient to future failures. Getting caught up on the awful feeling of failure holds you back. It ties you to the past, and it suffocates your future. Let your future breath by allowing it the energy it needs to survive hardship.

Trying to avoid failure ultimately doesn't accomplish anything. It takes work to accept failure, but doing so is a worthy endeavor. It does nothing for you to be afraid of failure. Dancing around failure means that you can't see the chances of success. You become so focused on what you didn't do that you can't see what you can do. It's not easy to become resilient to failure, but it is one of the most important skills in self-discipline. Self-disciplined people know that failures are a part of their experiences, but they are not their failures. Repeat after me, "I am more than more failures. I am the culmination of the times I've gotten up after my failures have knocked me down."

CHAPTER 7
Set Goals And Dream Big

Set Goals

Goal setting is one of the most important tasks that any person can do. A study by Harvard shows that only seventeen percent of the population has goals, and many of these people don't complete their goals and will have dropped them within a week. Other research shows that people who have goals are more likely to accomplish tasks, and the people who have goals are ten times more successful than the people who do not have goals. Thus, goal setting is an important part of being self-disciplined because it causes people to focus on what they want in the future rather than their immediate wants.

When you set goals, you feel like you are in charge of your future. You're given the keys to your future, and you are told that you get to choose what is behind the various doors that await you. When you set a goal, you take charge of your fate in the best way that you can. You do everything in your power to create the future that you want. Goal setters have more clarity because they don't have to worry as much about what may happen. They are mentally prepared for the future because they have the tools to deal with it. If you don't make goals, you cannot be self-disciplined because you will have nothing to stick to!

Goals help you create new habits. Habits are behaviors that unconsciously repeat because of having done them so many times before. They are your instinctual reaction to certain stimuli. For example, when you get ready in the morning, you may do so in a certain way— get up, have breakfast, brush your teeth, get ready, go to work, etc. When you set goals, you can better challenge your habits and enforce ones that help you out rather than ones that hurt you. Self-disciplined people can evaluate their habits, and when they see a problem habit, they set goals to break that habit.

Goals give you something to set your eyes on. They give you hopes to hang onto when life gets hard. When you feel lost, they give you a present reminder of what you want. Goals lead you to accomplishment, and they keep you from wandering too far. They allow some wandering but not enough that you forget what you've been looking for. Goals are a way to remain focused even though life is chaotic. By having a goal, there will be no questioning what you are trying to do, so you will more easily get what you want.

One thing that you should always do is write your goals down. Research widely shows that goals that are written down are more successful. You are one point four times more likely to complete a goal when you write it down versus when you don't. You are even more likely to complete that goal when you tell a friend about it. Both methods hold you accountable, and they make you feel more determined to see the goal through. If you just keep the goal to yourself, only in your brain, you can easily shrug it off or forget it entirely. Thus, making your goals known asserts to yourself that you mean business.

Set goals that are incremental and that you can measure. Incremental goals help you from getting overwhelmed. When you have just one big goal that far in the future, it can be easy to get complacent because it feels like that goal will never happen. If you want to lose 100 pounds in a year, don't just set that goal and be done with it. Set weekly goals so that you can see results immediately. Incremental goals serve as stepping stones to your larger goal. They keep you on track and ensure that you don't lose hope on your way towards your goal or quit. You also need to be able to measure your progress. Saying you want to do something until it "feels right" is vague and will be harder to stick to. Referring back to the weight example, losing 100 pounds is quantifiable. You can also use qualitative markers (as long as they are clear), but generally, people have the best results with quantifiable goals. Having goals is not enough; you also must have high-quality goals that set you up for success.

Setting goals allows you to accomplish tasks better than not setting goals. When you set goals, you make it obvious what you want to yourself, which makes it easier to stay on track. Self-disciplined people let their goals drive their actions, and they are sure to always have goals and create new goals as they complete old ones or decide they want something else. They also know how to set the right kind of goals, which are clear and don't leave room for wavering or backing out. They assert their wants, and they don't let themselves or others stand in the way of those wants.

Dream Big

Don't be afraid of your ambitions. Being ambitious is never a negative thing. Certain people can express their ambitions in obnoxious ways, but ambition itself isn't a bad thing. It's wonderful to dream big and have goals that are bolder than those of normal people. It is this ambition that creates innovation. The ability to push beyond expectations and strive to create something new is an incredible gift that self-disciplined people share. Self-disciplined people aren't content with what's safe or what's normal. They want to push boundaries and do something greater than most people can even imagine.

It's okay if you don't reach your dreams. The point is having something to strive for. Your incremental goals will be more manageable, but your big goal should be a major challenge. Dreaming doesn't cost you anything, so don't be afraid of hoping for things that you might not get. Don't let anyone discourage you from your dreams because while your dreams may seem silly to other people, they are important because they are yours. They are yours, and, understandably, you'd want to cherish them. Do your best to bring your dreams to life no matter what doubters say.

Let yourself dream. One of the most rewarding things a person can do is to dream. Dream challenges your imagination, and it allows you to explore ideas that other people haven't explored. Dreamers keep the world turning, and they are more content too. They embrace their imaginations. Too many adults lose sight of how remarkable their imaginations are. Let your imagination come alive, and don't be afraid of your creative side because creative expression is an important part of life.

CHAPTER 8
Convert Negativity Into Positivity

The Power of Positivity

Positive people lead better lives. Research shows that when you are positive, you have better psychological and health outcomes. One study by John Hopkins studied people who had a family history of heart problems. The results showed that people who used positive thinking were less likely to have a cardiac event. Further, they had better blood pressure and were less stressed. Thus, your attitude highly impacts how you will respond to situations. Self-disciplined people know that they won't get results from being negative.

Top-down processing shows how being positive can lead to behaviors that lead to better, more disciplined decisions. Top-down processing is the idea that people build expectations based on their endeavors and memories from their pasts. The top-level of information is the expectations, and once you have these expectations, you tend to create bottom-level information, which is your perceptions. To make this more clear, one experiment used red wine. One group was told that they had expensive wine while then they were told that they were drinking inexpensive wine. Both times they had the same wine, but those who had the "expensive" wine reported that it tasted better because they had higher expectations before drinking the wine. The parts of their brains that responded to pleasure also had increased activity when they drank the "expensive" wine. Thus, by putting positive expectations into your brain, you will respond more positively without making any changes. That is the power of positive thinking.

Because of the way their brains work, people who believe that they can do something are more likely to do that thing. If you believe that you can reach your goal, you're more likely to reach it. If you don't, you're more likely to turn to self-sabotaging behaviors. Your attitude can transform your entire life. You can go from being undisciplined to disciplined, just believing that you can do whatever you set your mind to. It doesn't require you to be a special kind of person because our brains all work similarly, and using that neuroscience, it's clear that changing what you input into your brain makes all the difference.

Don't doubt the power of a good attitude. When you're thinking positively, you can take on the world. Your worry decreases, and you believe in yourself. While some people like being pessimistic, pessimism isn't going to get you anywhere, so try to be a bit more positive, and you'll see that your life will change almost instantly.

Use Negativity for Good

When other people send negativity your way, use that negativity for good. You can use the negativity to fuel positivity. The more you resist the negativity, the easier it will be to stay on task and keep your head up when life gets arduous. Inevitably, you'll still feel negative sometimes, but the more you can stop yourself and turn that negativity into positive, the better. You don't need to let other people get you down with their words. It seems difficult to escape negativity with all the horrible things that happen in the world, but it's something you need to try to do for your own well being.

Make your own negatives into positives. Sometimes the negativity will be internal rather than external. When you feel negative about yourself, find ways to counteract those feelings. Maybe you don't like a feature on your body. Instead of focusing on that feature, focus on one that you like instead. Everyone has good parts of themselves, so if you can't think of one for yourself, you're in a deep negativity pit that you need to drag yourself out of. Negativity will never make you happy.

Don't let negativity become a defense mechanism. Some people use negativity as a shield from the bad things that might happen. They act pessimistic to protect themselves from the chance that their hopes might not come true. These people are the kind who struggle to try anything because they are so negative that they can't see good in the world or themselves. They sometimes frown upon positive people, but most pessimistic people are unhappy. They are all less happy than they could be. Pessimism can feel less scary than positivity, but it doesn't allow you to improve yourself or grow. A pessimistic person is like a flower being grown in a dark, dry basement with no TLC. Let yourself be in the sun! Feel the warmth on your skin, and let that light fuel you.

You can turn your negativity into positivity if you choose to do so. All you have to do is take that negativity and find bright sides to it. The bright sides don't have to be huge, but as long as you can find something good in the darkness, you'll be able to look at life through a positive lens. The more you practice positivity, the better you'll be at kicking negativity aside and swapping your outlook. Unfortunately, some people see positivity as naïve, but it's the healthiest outlook to have, and you can be positive without fooling yourself or being ignorant about serious issues. Positivity is about acknowledging the bad and trying to find a kernel of good to get yourself through the dark.

Learn to Relax

Relaxation is a vital part of your well-being and mental clarity. Self-disciplined people know that they can't work all the time, or they will get burnt out. Leisure and recreation are underestimated human needs. You cannot let your brain and body work all the time. They need time to breathe. There's nothing wrong with taking some time away from accomplishing. Sometimes, you do need a break because it is vital for your mental and physical health. Find time for yourself or with people who you love. Ensure that your need to relax is fulfilled fully. You'll never accomplish your goals if you push yourself too hard. You'll become tense, stressed, and be filled with negativity. Relaxation helps you take the time to return to a positive headspace, and it allows you to do things that you love without the pressure of having to reach certain goals. Not every area of your life needs to be goal-oriented. It's okay to leave some pursuits as just fun outlets and nothing more! Some people need more relaxation than others, so be sure to include as much or little as you need. Be honest with yourself, and if you need more relaxation time, don't feel like that makes you lazy.

CHAPTER 9
Remind Yourself Of Your Worth

The Issue of Self-Worth

Many people feel that they are not worthy of good things, and that feeling drives their life more than their desires do. Their identities become enwrapped in their doubts, and they lose track of what they most want. They think that all the good things that happen to them are underserved even when they have worked hard for them. They are fearful of all good things that come their way because when you have low self-worth, success can be scarier than outright failure because the more successful you are, the harder you fall when something goes wrong. Thus, by accomplishing little, the fear of failure is less crippling.

People have varying levels of self-esteem. All people have some doubts of some sort, but for healthy people, those doubts only pop up once in a while, and they do not prevent those people from taking chances and living their lives the way that they want to. Undisciplined people often are controlled by their low self-worth. They feel bound to fail, and they think that they cannot do anything right. This mentality is not only erroneous, but it is self-defeating. The more they convince themselves that they cannot do something, the less often people try that thing. They become unsuccessful people that their self-esteem told them they were.

Those with low self-esteem tend to struggle to self-discipline. When you have low self-worth, you struggle to allow good things to happen to you. You tend to back away when things start to go well. You take a back seat in your life, and you lose your ability to take control of your destiny. You become convinced that you will never have anything better than you have right now. You live less than content in your mediocrity, and while you feel discontent, you feel disempowered to do anything about it because of how awful you feel about yourself.

Why You Don't Feel Worthy

Self-esteem can be impacted by myriad factors. Factors such as how people grew up have a huge influence on people's self-esteem, but in many cases, societal factors and adolescence also have huge roles in the self-image of adults. All these factors join together and often make it hard for people to have confidence in themselves. Your self-worth could be based on how people treat you. Often, people who have been bullied or who have comments made on their bodies or other inherent qualities could develop insecurities about those aspects of themselves. You can internalize the messages sent by other people, which leads to insecurities. Insecurities could also be rooted in times when your survival felt threatened. For example, a sexual assault survivor may have self-worth issues because of the violation of their body. The list of why people don't feel worthy is endless. Jobs, intelligence, money, sexuality, power, marriage, friendships, and house are just a few of the things that can make people feel as though they are lesser, but of course, this list is not exhaustive.

Frequently, men, women, and non-binary people will have different experiences of insecurity based on the experiences they face because of their gender. Women, for example, often have self-esteem issues from an early age, and it quickly causes them problems. Women often have body insecurities and tend to blame other problems on their bodies. Among girls, seventy percent do not think that they are good enough. These negative feelings carry on into adulthood. Likewise, men have self-worth issues of their own. Many men are sensitive about their looks in ways unique to men. For example, men are more likely to feel insecure about being "scrawny" and are fixated on a muscular body ideal. They also may feel emasculated if they are not assertive as assertiveness is a trait that is often linked with masculinity. Non-binary people have their own unique issues that are oriented around the expectations for both men and women. Fitting in neither category completely can make finding their identity even harder, and it can result in additional insecurities. Evidently, no matter who you are, there are reasons that you have to be insecure. There are always aspects of life that will cause doubt.

People who society marginalizes may have extra self-worth issues. Black people, for instance, face prejudices that may make them feel lesser in a variety of ways. Similarly, LGBTQIA people may feel like outcasts for their sexualities, which will increase their self-doubt. These self-worth issues can increase problems like depression, anxiety, and eating disorders, which all lead to it being harder to have self-discipline.

Whatever reasons that you have for being insecure about, those insecurities have the power to drive your life in negative ways, which is why it helps to get a handle of your insecurities before they get out of control. Determine what makes you feel insecure so that you can address what makes you feel most inhibited.

How to Feel Worthy

Combat your insecurities. Challenge why you feel terrible about yourself, and try to discover ways that your doubts aren't true. Maybe you're convinced that you're an awful friend. Try instead to think of how you are a good friend. You may have areas to work on, but there are ways inherently that you must be a good friend, or else you wouldn't have any friends at all.

Find parts of yourself to love. No matter who you are, there are parts of yourself that you can love. Make a list of things that you like about yourself. Try to look beyond just bodily things too. Think about your personality and brain, and find things to like about those parts of yourself too. If you cannot think about anything you like, dig deeper. Don't feel like you have to be modest. There has to be at least one thing that you can like, at least tentatively, about yourself right now. Latch onto that thing, and as you learn to accept that one part, you can find others as well.

Focus on your strong areas. Stop thinking about the things that make you worthless, and start thinking about the things that give you worth. Take the things that are good about yourself, and run with those. You already know that being positive is important, so be positive about yourself too. Look in the mirror and find things to love because self-love is needed for self-discipline. If you don't love yourself, you won't listen to yourself.

Don't take the criticisms of others as automatic truth. Sometimes, other people may have a valid criticism of you, but don't assume that you are what other people say that you are. If someone calls you stupid, don't automatically think, "Yes, I am stupid." Use your critical thinking to determine what you really are. No one is stupid. We all just have areas that we are smarter about, and that's okay. That's how it should be because we can balance each other out.

CHAPTER 10
Don't Blame Others And Maintain Good Relationships

Don't Blame Others

It can be easy to blame other people for your lack of self-discipline. You don't want to feel bad about yourself, so you find other people to cast the blame on. You're working on a group project that goes wrong, and you say, "But Sue..." and you list all the ways that the error had nothing to do with you. Granted, often, other people are to blame, but blaming other people for failures that are rightly yours doesn't help you. When a project has failed, you must take your portion of the blame. You must know how to see, "Yes, Sue did this, but I could have done that better." When you work with others, you share blame for things that go wrong, and when you work by yourself, there's no reason to point the finger at anyone else! Things will go wrong that won't be your fault, but even then, you have to say, "I didn't realize everything, and I was unable to live up to the expectations that I had." This statement doesn't make you a bad person. It just makes you a person.

Other people aren't responsible for your success. When you don't take responsibility for your own life, you cannot be self-disciplined. Thus, you shouldn't attribute either your successes or failures to other people. Get out of the mindset that you are a passive force in your own life. You are the active force of your life. You have the power to make your own decisions and fix your own problems. It is great to have people who are willing to help you, and there's nothing wrong with asking for help, but be ready to face your mistakes alone if it comes down to that.

Other people will wrong you, but it doesn't help you to blame all your misfortune on them. You're not going to change the situation by pointing a finger at other people. Sure, it can feel temporarily vindicating to blame other people, but it's better to solve the problem immediately rather than wasting time trying to figure out who was the source of the problem. When you have to blame others, you are not doing yourself any justice because you are dismissing yourself as an active participant in the project.

Maintain Good Relationships

Relationships are an important part of life, and they can help determine whether you can be self-disciplined or not. When you have strong relationships, you are happier, and having a support system helps keep you accountable. Good people will motivate you to stick to your goals. They will convince you not to give up. They will believe in you when you struggle to believe in yourself. Those people can give you the extra push that you need when you're feeling down. They will make or break your goal-reaching. Plus, success is no fun when there's no one around to celebrate with!

Romantic and platonic relationships are both important unless you are not aromatic and are not interested in romantic relationships. For the majority of people, a balance between romantic, familial, and platonic relationships are necessary to remain healthy. Ensuring that you give everyone fair attention helps you maintain your various relationships. It can be easy to get lost in certain relationships to the point that you neglect others and lose your balance. To keep them healthy, you need to ensure that your relations are good for everyone involved. Your relationships should be mutually beneficial. You need to have relationships with people who don't want to hold you back, and you shouldn't want to hold your friends or other loved ones back either. You should both benefit from knowing each other, and you should give as much as you take.

Relationships need to be dynamic. Some relationships can last years or even decades, and those relationships can't stay the same. Your parents, for example, should treat you differently when you're an adult versus when you are a child. Your parents shouldn't be telling you what shoes you should be wearing as a forty-year-old like they would when you were three. Relationships need to be appropriate for your development, and they need to respond to crucial changes in your life. Friendships, for instance, won't look the same when you have kids, and that's fine. You just need to know how to adapt to that and let the relationship change as you do.

You should have different relationships that are different based on what that relationship is. You shouldn't expect your relationship with your mother to feel the same as your relationship with your best friend. Relationships have unique dynamics, and you should embrace those dynamics. Learn to love what makes each relationship what it is. Don't strive to replicate what you have with one person with other people. Treating people differently doesn't mean that you love them more or less. It just means that that person needs something different from you than other relationships do or you need something from them. Relationships don't need to be identical, and having ones that look different can provide more diverse support when you need it. Sometimes, you need a tough-love friend, and sometimes you need a commiseration friend.

When you have a relationship, ensure that it is not toxic. No relationship should be crippling to your self-esteem. If it is, it is time to address that relationship and to make changes. If you don't feel safe or happy in a relationship, you can't continue acting the same way and avoiding all that feels wrong. Some relationships won't be salvageable, and there's nothing wrong with having to let go. It is hard to let go, but sometimes you have to for your own well-being. You're never obligated to continue a relationship. You can break a relationship with your own mother if it isn't making you feel good about yourself and your life. You need to ensure your mental health and have people who will do good things for you, not bad. Relationships are never easy, but good ones will always be more good than bad.

Remember that you are part of your relationships. You cannot expect one person to carry all the weight. You cannot carry the relationship all by yourself, and neither can the other person. Relationships are all about balancing needs. Sometimes you will need your friend, and sometimes they will need you. Being selfish and not paying attention to the other person's needs will destroy that relationship, and it will result in unnecessary friction that will distract you from your goals. You'll never thrive if you make the relationship all about you or if you never share any problems with your friends. Don't act as though you are around the people you care about. Be vulnerable and show multiple sides to you. No one wants a robot for a friend, nor do they want someone who is totally self-obsessed.

Social experiences are a vital part of human life, and depriving yourself of strong relationships will put you in a bad mental space. When you have good, strong relationships, you can look at life more positively and are less likely to worry about other people. A strong social life allows you to push through hardship more easily. People with good interpersonal relationships are more resilient to stress and can more easily find success. Do not try to persevere on your own. No matter how self-disciplined you are, it is hard to accomplish anything if you isolate yourself. Put some TLC into your relationships to make sure that they endure and are there when you need them.

CHAPTER 11
Remember That Success Isn't Stagnant

You Won't Always Be the Same

People never stay the same. There are some qualities that we inherently have, but these qualities are shaped by our circumstances. You may be inherently shy, but you won't be shy in all circumstances. You can probably find ways to reduce the impact of your shyness on social circumstances. You can push yourself to be less shy, even if you can't erase that shyness. The point is that while your personality doesn't change, the way that you express that personality will change as you learn and (hopefully) grow. There's no point in trying to stay stagnant in time. Time will go on, and you will get older, whether you like it or not.

You're not the same as you were ten years ago. Think about yourself ten years ago, and I think you'll be able to tell that you aren't the same person. You've probably had major life changes— marriage, kids, graduations, new pets, death. Those circumstances have inevitably impacted you and your lifestyle. Even tiny changes can have a huge impact on how you interact with the world and how you view yourself. Ten years ago, you might have been a worse person. You might have been a better person, but whoever you were, that person won't define who you are or who you will be.

You won't be the same ten years from now. Many more things will happen in ten years, and you can't predict where life will take you. You don't know who will die or who will be born. People could get sick. People could get better. There's so much that you can squeeze into ten years, and you'll feel very differently in those ten years versus how you feel now. You'll want different things, and you'll have different physical and mental needs. You'll still be yourself, but in many ways, you will be different.

Embrace the changes that are to come. The changes should be exciting more than they are scary. Change allows you to improve your life, and it prevents you from getting bored. Without change, there would be no point in living. Change gives you something to look forward to even in the darkest of situations. You don't always like the changes, but you can always embrace them. You can accept even the worst things that happen to you and let them guide you without knocking you off course. Respect the changes and use them to your advantage.

Know that you'll be successful as long as you commit to yourself. When you commit to yourself, you become more resilient. You can commit to remaining true to yourself no matter what changes in your life. You can decide that you will remain self-assured even when life throws doubt at you. You must learn to be resistant to the negative energies that will try to disarm you and convince you to give up. The changes are just circumstances, and when those circumstances happen, they don't change who you are. You're still the amazing you!

Your Situation May Change Mid-Ambition

You can start a journey and realize that it's not what you want. Because we cannot know the future, we cannot always know what we'll want even one week from now. That doesn't mean that we should keep postponing change. All that means is that we need to stay cognizant of our fickle nature as human beings. Your wants can change in a snap, and these changes are often provoked by changes in your circumstances. You know that situations change. You go from being unencumbered to having new responsibilities that you might not be ready for. You are forced to make changes that you didn't plan on having to make.

Sometimes, your priorities will change. You will realize that what you thought was important wasn't that important. Maybe you go from worrying about the way your body looks. You throw yourself into a workout regime. You're working out so much that you barely see your family, but then, your dad gets sick. He has terminal cancer, and suddenly, working out seems less important than spending time with your dad. You stop worrying so much about how many squats you can do, and you start taking measures to make your dad's last months special. These changes don't mean you have a lack of self-discipline. They only mean that you had to make adjustments.

Life will throw you curveballs, and they'll strike you out. You won't always hit home runs as nice as that will be. Sometimes, you'll be tossed back, and you'll fall on your butt. You'll go through things that will hurt you. You'll break your arm, and you'll have to step back from what you were doing. These curveballs represent just one inning of your life, and unlike baseball, you have far more than nine innings. Just because you lose one round doesn't mean you lose everything. There's still plenty of chances to do better. All you have to do is take them instead of letting them take you.

What was possible yesterday might not be possible today. Things that were feasibly accomplishable yesterday may not be viable today. For example, if you want to prevent diabetes by eating healthier, being diagnosed with diabetes might make that goal impossible. Nevertheless, that's not an excuse to give up. Even if you get diabetes, you can still make changes that will reduce the symptoms or even reverse diabetes. You'll have to shift what is possible rather than invalidating it all together.

What was impossible yesterday might be possible today. Maybe yesterday the job you wanted didn't have an opening, but today, there's a new opening for the position you wanted. If you're patient, the opportunities that you want may present themselves. As you wait, you can work to put yourself in the best position for the chances that you want. Work on the skills that the job you want would require, even if the job isn't available yet. That way, when the job is available, you'll be more likely to get it. Sometimes, you'll have to wait for things to be possible, but that doesn't mean you can't take steps to ensure success regarding those things while you wait.

Life works at a rapid pace, which can make it hard to stick to the plan. Life breezes on by sometimes. It can be hard to catch all the chances that fly your way while dodging all the blows. You may feel unhinged and out of control because of how quickly your situation changes. One day, you have a nice job, and the next day you could be fired. I don't say that to scare you. Rather, I say that because there's no point fearing the rapidness of life. Instead, you should try to let the rapid pace give you momentum. Let the changes be what propels you forward.

It's Okay to Change Your Mind

It's easy to realize that what you thought you wanted isn't what you want at all. Beyond just your circumstances changing, sometimes you'll have access to new information that will change your entire perspective on a certain situation. You'll realize that what you thought was right was wrong. It will dawn on you that you should've been doing something completely different than what you are doing. Sometimes, it will strike you suddenly; you'll pause in your tracks and want to go a different way. There's nothing wrong with that.

With the changes in life, new light may be cast and change your perspective. We go through much of our lives in dim lighting. We can only see a little portion of our path, which makes it hard to make good decisions when we initially make them. We end up wandering more than we would like, and as we wander, new areas become bright. We realize that what we thought was true wasn't true completely. We see new perspectives. We interact with other people who may show us views we never even considered. Sometimes, we realize that we have to change our minds to fit the people who we want to be.

It's okay to change your mind, but don't change your mind merely because of fear. It can be easy to become indecisive in the face of fear. You freeze, and you start to back out, excusing your indecision away with the comment that, "I'm just changing my mind." Changing your mind is not an excuse to hide behind. When it is genuine, okay, but when you want to change your mind, ask yourself why you're changing your mind, and if it is because you are scared with no other reason, reevaluate your decision to back out. If you always change your mind, you'll never get anywhere.

Changing your mind does not mean admitting defeat. It's wise to know when you need to stop or pause. Sometimes, it's vital to your growth as a person to do so. Part of being self-disciplined is being honest with yourself when you want to make changes. It is knowing whether you are changing your mind for the right reasons, and it is knowing when sticking to what you're trying to do will only hurt you in the long run.

You Define Success

At the end of the day, you are the sole authority on your success. Success means whatever you want it to be. Society will try to tell you what it thinks that success should be, but often, that perspective is narrow minded, and it isn't meant for your exact circumstances. No one understands what you've had to go up against quite like you, so what you see as a victory may not be a victory to them. Don't rely on what society tells you is a success because you can never be successful if you judge yourself on parameters created for idyllic people who check certain boxes.

No one can tell you that you are not successful if you think you are. When you feel satisfied with your accolades, it no longer matters what other people think of your success. When you determine that something is an achievement, it is an achievement. For some people, getting a C on a paper would feel like a failure, while for others, that would feel like a victory. Just because someone else would see that C as a failure doesn't mean that is. If you struggled in a class and managed to get a C, that is a victory that you should be proud of. Success doesn't require comparison to anyone other than your past self.

Success means different things to different people. Just as in the example with the C paper, people don't always have the same point of view on what success is, so you cannot take the views of others too seriously. There's no need to feel bad just because someone looks down upon your success. You should still feel proud of what you've done because of the work you put in and the obstacles that you had to encounter to get to where you are. Naysayers are everywhere, and they will never make you feel self-assured, and they certainly won't help you become more self-disciplined. You can be more successful if you change your outlook. Maybe it isn't other people who are being too critical of you. Maybe you are being too critical of yourself. When that's the case, you will never be satisfied. Anything that you do will never be enough, and you will drive yourself crazy with expectations that you cannot reasonably live up to. If you don't let yourself be happy when you do well and instead poke holes in your accomplishment by saying, "I did well, but..." then you are not in the right frame of mind to have any autonomy over yourself. You are giving up on yourself, which is the worst thing that you can do.

Having self-discipline is knowing how to accept your own version of success. Find what makes you happy, and that is a success. Success doesn't mean being the best. It doesn't mean winning. It doesn't mean doing the impossible. Success means persevering and doing your best. It means fighting through your self-doubts. It means being true to yourself even when it is hard. Success is letting yourself keep striving for a better life. It is keeping a good attitude and working hard for what you want. Ultimately, success is whatever you decide it to be, so decide carefully.

CHAPTER 12
Don't Say You'll Try, Say You'll Do

The Fallacy of Trying

People often say that they will try, but when they use the word "try," they often don't end up trying that hard. They give a half-hearted effort that results in disappointment. When you say that you will, you usually do not say so with confidence. You say it with a seed of doubt that gives you an out for when you don't want to try anymore. The word try is an excuse for people who aren't willing to commit to their goals. It is a weak word that promises someone will do their best, but it doesn't hold them accountable to actually do their best.

Trying means that you half believe that you will not succeed. When you say that you will do something, you are affirming that you fully believe that you are going to do it, but "try" gives you an out for failure. You can say, "I tried my best," even if you gave up. Instead of trying, you need to just do it. Self-discipline is committing fully. It is knowing that you might fail, but it is giving your all regardless. It is asserting your desire to do your best, and it is leaving no room for doing something halfway.

The fallacy of trying is that when you say that you will try, you are being too cautious. You are backing away from trying because you're afraid of failing. Doing something requires risk, but trying something can result in quitting. When you get a free trial, you don't have to lose your money if you don't like it. It's completely risk-free. Don't let your life be a free trial. You're worth more than that.

Why You Need to Do

You need to give your all to your attempts. If you don't give your all, it's easier to quit. If you give less than everything to an attempt, you're setting yourself up for failure. You're using your half efforts as a safety net. You'll never reach your potential if you do everything in halves. When you give your all, you can never regret not giving enough because you'll know that you did your best. You didn't just try. You took every opportunity, and you put your aspirations into action.

Don't accept trying from yourself. Stop trying right now. Take action and take charge of your life. Don't waver on your goals. Decide what you want to do, and use strong language when you assert your goals. Know that you can do better. No matter what you are doing right now, you can push yourself to do better. It's your life, and you can do whatever you set your mind to, but if you settle for just trying, you will try until the day that you die.

Tell yourself that you are going to do it. You are not going to back out. You are not going to quit. You are not going to go halfway. You are going to embrace your potential, and you are going to be self-disciplined. You aren't going to try to be self-disciplined. You're not going to waver. You are going to do it! When you believe that you can do it, you are more likely to. There's nothing shameful about doing, even if your action doesn't culminate in the results that you want.

CHAPTER 13
Sleep, Exercise, And Food

Sleep, exercise, and diet are all factors that influence your ability to be self-disciplined. If you don't have balance in these areas of your life, your body and your mind will not be healthy enough to maintain self-discipline. They will start to rebel against you and resist any efforts that you make to change. All three are sources of difficulty for many people, but if you invest some time and energy into exploring how these areas impact you, you can improve any of these areas in your life, which will provide the mental clarity and physical health you need for self-discipline.

Sleep

Sleep is one of the most important needs that you need to fulfill to keep yourself on track with any goal. People often neglect their need to sleep. They think that they are too busy to waste eight hours with their eyes closed. This misinformed thinking does more harm than good because it decreases people's abilities to function and complete tasks as they would normally. When you are tired, your work becomes more sloppy, and your mood dips. You're less productive when you're sleepy, and it's harder to start new things. All you want to do is crawl back in bed rather than living to your potential.

Sleep does miraculous things for your physical health. Research shows that people who get eight hours of sleep live longer. They are more resistant to chronic conditions as well as conditions like heart disease and cancer. Being well-rested gives the body time to recharge itself and heel. It allows your bodily functions to run more optimally. Further, it ensures that you don't push yourself past your limits. The body does several vital processes while you sleep, so if you aren't sleeping well, your body doesn't get to accomplish all that it needs to, so it runs on fumes and sputters along as you go through your day.

Sleep is also good for your mental health. People who don't get sleep feel grumpy. They also have a worse overall outlook on life. They are more likely to be stressed, angry, anxious, or depressed. When you are tired, you're more irritable. When any little thing goes wrong, it may feel like the end of the world when you're tired. Being exhausted makes it hard to deal with other people, and you may find yourself unable to concentrate on important tasks. There are few things as draining as trying to get through a day without enough sleep.

Ultimately, sleep allows you to function more optimally in all areas of your life. It makes you more resistant to hardship, and it makes you feel calmer. Not only do you need an ample amount of sleep, but you need good quality sleep. Many people wake up frequently during the night or are light sleepers. If that is the case for you, try investigating the root of your sleep problems and try to address it as well as you can. Unfortunately, it can be hard to find sleep solutions, but a little research and logging your sleep patterns can help you learn how to get a better night's sleep. The more you study your own sleep, the better information you'll have to make adjustments.

If you don't have sleep, you will not have the mental or physical well-being needed to be disciplined with yourself. Sleep is not an optional part of life. People need to sleep. Without sleep, they slowly lose functioning. Being tired can have the same impacts on your responses as being under the influence of alcohol. Thus, trying to function while you're tired will never bring the results that you crave. Nobody likes being tired, so don't be too busy to sleep. Make time to get your eight hours in so that you feel refreshed.

Exercise

Exercise may not seem that exciting to you, but it is important in establishing a routine of self-discipline. It's easier to be self-disciplined when you are taking care of your body. Unfortunately, too few people are getting adequate exercise that they need to function optimally. Less than five percent of American people get at least half an hour of exercise per day, and eighty percent do not get enough aerobic or strengthening workouts. People are failing to be active, which leads to health consequences, both physical and mental.

Exercise is good for both your physical and mental health. Exercise helps people keep their blood pressure under control. It also reduces bad cholesterol and makes people more resistant to heart disease and cancer. It can also be good for your immune health. Further, exercise is one of the best ways to keep your mood level. It can lessen the symptoms of depression and ease anxiety. Further, it sends a rush of feel-good chemicals through your body that makes you feel better about yourself and happier too. Regular exercise also can help you sleep better. Further, it regulates your hunger chemicals, leptin, and ghrelin, which allows you to eat better. Exercise has a huge impact on your health, and it creates a domino effect by allowing so many areas of your health to improve by just adding a little activity.

Find ways of exercising that make you feel good about yourself and that you enjoy. If you don't like doing something, there's no point in forcing yourself to do it. There's a type of exercise that can appeal to any person. You may have to put in some work to find what works best for you, but when you finally find something that you can enjoy at least on some level, you will feel a lot better about exercising. Exercising will always be hard work, but it doesn't have to be something that you dread. Lots of fun exercising programs like ones that include dance can barely feel like exercise at all! Even just a nice walk through nature can be a great way to incorporate more exercise into your life.

Food

The food you eat will make a difference in how you feel. Ensure that you are eating all types of macronutrients (carbs, proteins, and fats) as well as micronutrients (vitamins and minerals). Try not to eat over processed foods that are nutritionally hollow because these may bog you down and make you feel sluggish and unmotivated. A balanced diet keeps your head clear, and your body functioning as it should. The goal of your diet is not to limit what you eat and prohibit certain foods. Rather, you should try to eat more things that will make you feel good to promote a better lifestyle overall.

Don't be afraid of carbs. With diet culture being so popular, people often vilify carbs. They think that carbs will cause weight gain and health problems, and this view isn't nuanced. You do want to limit simple carbohydrates— processed sugars and non-whole grains— but complex carbs are vital for your health. Your brain uses carbs as its source of energy. While you can convert other energy into ketones in a process called ketosis, eating carbs is the ideal way to fuel your brain. Foods like whole grain rice or whole wheat pasta can be great ways to feel less hungry and to sustain your energy. Simple carbs like cookies or chips will give you a burst of energy, but then, you will shortly have a crash because those simple carbs have had several parts of the grain kernel removed, making them less satiating. Complex carbs are more nutritionally dense, meaning that they give you more nutrients and keep you full longer.

Proteins are your friends. Protein is great for your muscles, joints, and a myriad of other bodily functions. Protein does a lot for your body, and it can be found in sources like meat, dairy, eggs, soy, and some other combined foods (like rice and beans). Protein keeps you feeling strong, and it also helps you to stay satiated. Just like it's important to have carbs, you need to have a balance of proteins too, preferably eating them throughout the day because you can't store excess proteins in your body and have to replenish your supplies throughout the day. Lean proteins like chicken and tuna are often considered to be the healthiest for you but don't be afraid to eat whatever proteins you like in moderation.

Monounsaturated and polyunsaturated fats are good for you. These fats allow you to absorb fat-soluble vitamins like A, E, D, and K. Fat is often vilified like carbs. People don't want to become "fat." While some fats, like trans and saturated fats, can have negative health results such as increased bad cholesterol, certain healthy fats can have reverse impacts. They can increase your good cholesterol and decrease your bad cholesterol. Good fats can be found in foods like olive oil, sunflower oil, canola oil, flaxseed oil, almonds, avocados, and cold water fish. Omega-

3 and Omega-6 supplements may help you balance your healthy fat levels as well.

Vitamins and minerals are essential parts of any diet. These substances can be found in many foods, especially fruits and vegetables. They play a variety of roles in your body, so they keep all your organs and bodily systems running smoothly. If you don't have these foods, you will feel sick, and your body will suffer in many ways. All your systems will work less optimally, depending on your deficiencies. You may experience changes in your skin, vision, and muscles. Ensure that your plate is filled with a variety of colors to ensure that you get all the nutrients that you need. Up your fruit and vegetable intake to make sure that you get the nutrients that you need. Supplements can also be effective, but your body does not absorb them as well as it does through the natural food source. Though, anything is better than nothing when it comes to vitamins and minerals.

Your diet doesn't need to be restrictive and eliminate foods you love, but adding more healthy foods can help you feel better. Having a balanced diet is not only good for your body, but it is good for your mind. When you are all around healthy, you can commit to self-discipline because you have the physical and mental tools that you need to commit to bettering yourself. If you feel awful, it will be hard to stick to anything.

CHAPTER 14
If You Hate It, Change It

When you don't like something, you're never going to excel at that thing, which is why you need to stop forcing yourself to do things that don't make you feel happy. Start doing things that challenge you and make you feel fulfilled instead. The more you do what you like, the less burdensome it will feel to have self-discipline.

Self-Discipline Doesn't Mean Dread

Self-discipline shouldn't mean that you force yourself to do things that you hate. Self-discipline is hard to come by if you can find no joy in your activity. Doing things that you hate is one of the most unmotivating activities that you can do. Research shows that when people do things that they hate, they are less likely to complete their tasks, and they take longer to complete them. When you don't like your job or your exercise regime, you will feel tortured as you do it. You'll be counting the days until it is over rather than enjoying the journey of getting to your goal.

If your aspirations are things that you hate, you aren't being true to yourself. You're trying to be someone who you wish you were instead of yourself. It shouldn't feel like a burden to strive for your goals. It should feel exciting. There will always be part of your work that you don't like, but you need to find things in that work that are exciting and fulfilling for you, or you will never better yourself. You'll feel stuck with no release, you'll wish for change without knowing how to create it.

What You Do Should Bring You Joy

Self-discipline is meant to be applied to things that you enjoy. Self-discipline is just masochism when you do it for things that make you feel like a machine. That doesn't mean that things you find challenging can't have any joy. I hate running, but I still enjoy the process of challenging myself when I completed my first race. While there was much about running that I didn't enjoy, there were still times when I found enjoyment, and those were the parts that helped me reach my goal of partaking in a charity race. There's no sense in sticking out things that make you hate your life.

Gritting your teeth and pushing through something is sometimes required, but you need to find bright spots in anything you do. Find areas of your life that fill you with joy if some bring you heaps of dread. Work to bring fulfillment to everything that you do. There's nothing worse than doing something that feels hollow. It doesn't make you feel alive. It makes you feel like a zombie, walking deadly through life while still resembling a living being. Some people may not be in a position where they can easily change. Sometimes, you have the job you have because there are no other ones available that meet your needs but find ways to work towards goals that will better your position.

Don't Be Afraid to Push Your Boundaries

If you feel stuck in place, you probably aren't going anywhere. Listen to your feelings and let them tell you when you need to emerge from your comfort zone. Boundaries are meant for breaking. Don't see your boundaries and walk in circles until the day you die. Take tasks that people said you couldn't do, and do them. Your boundaries give you an illusion of safety, but they will suffocate if you let them. They will take all your life force, and make you think that you can't feel any happier than you do right now. They will convince you that you are not worth anything more. They will smother you until you sink under the weight of your stillness.

Don't be content with the status quo. The status quo is what society tells you is right. It is the expectations that have been put on you by the culture that surrounds you. The status quo isn't always what best fits your needs, though. Who cares if you want to wear white after Labor Day? Challenge those expectations and do what makes you feel content. Does it really matter that much if society says that you need to change your body? No, it doesn't. You don't need to change yourself to fit the ideals that other people have made. As long as you strive to be a good person, there's no need to try to fit any molds that society has provided.

Challenge what you know. What you know may be logically inconsistent. Sometimes, you have prejudices that you may be unaware of. Don't be afraid of your ignorance. There's nothing wrong with ignorance other than the unwillingness to learn. You can grow through what you don't know. Maybe you were raised to think that it was wrong to be gay. Ask yourself if that idea matches your other beliefs. Do you really think gayness is wrong, or is that what society tells you? The answer you reach is up to you, but it is important to challenge your beliefs because it is through doubts that you reaffirm and shift your values.

Be able to admit when you are wrong. When you have wronged someone, be mature and fess up to it. Don't try to list all the ways that you were right. Don't let your pride get in your way of doing the right thing. Your ignorance can be changed. You can learn to be wise, and that's part of getting older. It's learning that sometimes you will be wrong, but being wrong shouldn't send you spiraling off course. You shouldn't give up when you misinterpret a situation. Instead, you should use the knowledge you have found to redirect yourself.

No one loves stagnancy. Some people fall into the stagnancy trap. They are lulled by its false sense of security, but if you continue to not go anywhere in life, you are never going to feel the satisfaction that you would have if you had self-discipline. Movement requires being honest with yourself and admitting that you will make mistakes sometimes, but it is one of the best feelings that you will ever have.

CHAPTER 15
Be Open To New Things

Be Bolder

It's easy to tell you to push your boundaries, but how can you be more open to new things? It's not as easy as it sounds, but the simplest answer is to be bolder. Don't be afraid to do things that you would never have done before. Challenge who you are. Challenge who you want to be. Whoever it was who you were yesterday, try to be someone better. Take any chance; you have to be courageous with your identity and with the way that you present yourself to the rest of the world. It is liberating to show yourself to others, so don't hide who you are, and don't feel ashamed of your dreams or interests.

Try things that are "out of character." Sometimes, people tend to limit themselves based on their reputations. Someone who historically claimed that they hated watching football, might feel weird admitting that they like football several years later. It seems strange that people would feel ashamed of wanting to evolve, but it can feel like your identity is being questioned when you change your mind. Sometimes, you're too stubborn to enjoy that you like things because you feel like you should hate them. Reality TV shows are guilty pleasures for many people who feel like they are too mature or smart to enjoy such TV, but there are no good reasons for being ashamed of liking things just because you hated them a year ago. It helps you grow to try things that you thought weren't for you.

Don't force yourself into a box. You are more than your job. You are more than your relationships with people. You are more than your hobbies. You cannot be reduced down to just one thing that you are. Embrace that you are multifaceted and that you are a person full of contradictions. We all have ways that we don't make sense. We all have interests or tastes that seem to clash, but that is how humans are, and there's no reason to shove us into boxes and try to fit certain molds.

Assert yourself more often. When people try to demean you for who you are, stand up for yourself and your interests. Don't let other people invalidate for things that give you joy so long as those actions don't hurt others. Whoever you are, whatever you like, is valid. You deserve to have passions without being mocked. Society likes to mock certain things that it doesn't understand. For example, people with intense passion may be mocked for "being too much," and loving the things that they love too strongly. Don't let people put out your fire. Burn brighter and remain passionate because that passion sets you apart from everyone else.

Listen to others. Listening often doesn't seem bold, but getting past your ego to listen to others can be one of the boldest things that you can do.

Just as you should assert yourself, you should let others assert themselves too. Listen to their passions rather than judging them. Judgment closes you off to forming relationships, and it makes you more judgmental about yourself. Often, judgments you make about people are judgments that you've internalized. The things that you don't like in other people are the things that you often don't like in yourself. Don't destroy the passions of other people because when you destroy their passions, you are hurting yourself. You are impeding your own success by closing your heart and your mind.

Being bold means having the courage to fight for your beliefs and to learn in new ways. It doesn't mean talking over people or bullying them to believe the same things that you do. It means being sure about yourself without belittling others. You should be free to love what you love as should other people. You should be able to pursue your passion without shame. That takes courage. It takes the boldness that so few people have. It is the self-discipline that so many people lack.

What's the Worst That Can Happen?

Thoughts about worst-case scenarios often invoke fear in us and make us hesitant to change. They make us feel that moment of being overwhelmed and invoke panic. When you think of the worst, you start to fear. All your doubts come alive, and they become the worst kinds of monsters. They're big, ugly, and seem unbeatable. They make you cower in a corner, wanting to curl up and cry. You start to think that the reward of your chances is not worth the risks. You become paralyzed by your own doubts, and you think that there is no way that you can overcome all the possibilities that stand in your way.

Let yourself imagine the worst-case scenarios. Don't try to ignore the worries that are bubbling up in your mind because if you are ignoring what is worrying you, you aren't facing those fears. You're trying to make them go away, and that doesn't help you make sense of them. You need to think about the worst that can happen because that will help you cope with your anxiety. It will give you a new perspective. It's hard to see anything clearly as the world blurs around you as you run away.

The worst that can happen probably isn't as bad as you think. If you're worried about a work project, you probably fear that if you don't do well that you will get fired. The idea of being fired consumes you to the point that you don't want to start the project. More realistically, making a small mistake isn't going to get you fired, so if you take the time to do the project as well as you can, you're not going to fail that much, and if you do, there's not much that you can do to change that failure. You can only do as much as you can do, and you must learn to be okay with that.

When you imagine the worst, you realize that the chances of good things happening are more likely. You start to see that the panic you felt was just your imagination going wild. When you expect the world to explode, usually, you usually just have a few sparks. When you try to run away from the things that fear you, you end up procrastinating, and when you procrastinate, you have less time to complete what you want to accomplish. Thus, you end up doing worse quality work. Accordingly, facing your fears can kick your anxiety before you end up quitting whatever it is that you are trying to do.

CHAPTER 16
Accept Criticism

Constructive Criticism Is Necessary.

In life, you will inevitably be criticized. Constructive criticism is part of dealing with other people. There will always be people who have bad things to say about what you are doing, and because you are not perfect, some of that criticism is warranted. Criticism doesn't have to ruin your day. You can learn to accept it and to live with it rather than letting it get you down because you need criticism to grow as a person.

Criticism Doesn't Mean You're Worthless

When you are given constructive criticism, it doesn't mean that there's something inherently wrong with you. Criticism is usually given with your best interests in mind. It is meant to help you adjust your course and do better. While some people will give you criticism to be rude, most will want the best for you, so don't take it as a personal assault.

You are distinct from your work product. You are much more than just one piece of feedback or even multiple pieces of feedback. Surely, there are things that you did right, probably more than you did wrong. Criticism of a project doesn't mean that you are a bad person, a bad employee, a bad parent, etc. It just means you have areas that you can improve upon. Further, criticism is often just opinions. What one person thinks is a weak point in your work will be a strong point for someone else. People's opinions are meant to guide you rather than dictating what you will do. You decide what you will make of your criticism.

Criticism Helps You Grow

We all need criticism because, without it, we would stagnate as people. It would make us all afraid of trying to learn things that we don't fully understand. Criticism gives us a wider perspective. It shows us that there are other views of the world than our own. It alerts us to details that we might have never thought about otherwise. It helps us strengthen whatever we are doing, and it helps us strengthen ourselves.

The more you learn to be okay with criticism, the less defensive you get, and the more you can learn. When you can be told that you may be wrong and look at it through an analytical lens rather than an emotional one, you can better judge the validity of the criticism rather than just waving it away as if it doesn't matter. Not all criticism is right, but it helps you be self-disciplined when you can consider all criticism that comes your way. Criticism can be intimidating, but self-disciplined people know that it is part of progress. No one moves forward without criticism.

When you are given constructive criticism, you are being shown that you are worth the effort required to give feedback. When people critique you, they are usually saying that they believe in your work. They are asserting that you were worth the time it took to go over your work.

CHAPTER 17
The World Isn't Ending

The Catastrophic Tendency

Calm down, Chicken Little, the sky isn't falling. People experience obstacles, and then they shut down. They become convinced that they cannot handle the hardships of their lives, and they back off. They turn away from self-discipline and act with cowardice. They give up on trying anything because they are so scared that they might walk outside and see that the world is ending.

It's easy for people to expect the worst in life. When you catastrophize, you stress yourself out for no reason. The more you catastrophize, the harder it becomes to cope. You start to see issues in every little thing. Your own shadow feels like a threat. When things don't go perfectly, you break down and wonder if you'll ever do anything right. Stop looking at all the wrong, and start looking at all the opportunities that you will have by taking some researched chances.

How to Avoid Catastrophizing

Return to our worst-case scenario exercise. Remember that the worst isn't likely to be the thing that happens. Take a deep breath and kick your anxiety away because it won't help you. Know that if things go wrong, it isn't the end of the world. You're going to be able to handle whatever comes your way because you have the skills you need to persevere. You will be self-disciplined, and you will not give up on your dreams because things might go wrong. You will learn to handle the little bumps in the road because those bumps will lead to satisfaction.

As long as you're alive, you have the chance to move on from your mistakes. Mistakes shouldn't be seen as failures. Mistakes are the best opportunities that you will get to grow. The more you accept your mistakes, the less they will bother you. Mistakes happen every day. Even the greatest people of all people have made mistakes, but those mistakes didn't stop them. They pushed through the mistakes to make themselves better. Tiger Woods wasn't born a great golfer. He had to work to be great, and in his golfing comeback, he had to drag himself from darkness and hardship to return to greatness.

Take breaths when you feel panic coming on. Take a moment to step back and look at the situation as if you were an outsider. If you were someone else, would you feel as worried? If you were just a bystander, would you be expecting that your mistake or obstacle was the end of the world? Probably not. You would be able to see that what you were dealing with was something that you had all the skills to handle.

Know that it's okay to feel overwhelmed, but it's not okay to get carried away with that feeling. Everyone gets overwhelmed sometimes. Accept that feeling and respect it, but don't let it drive you to the point of insanity. Resist that negativity and try to replace it with positivity. It is natural to catastrophize, but it is also natural to pause and stop the feelings that are overwhelming you. You do not have to be controlled by your feelings. You can determine how they impact your actions.

CHAPTER 18
Learn To Embrace Your Unconscious Mind

Your unconscious thoughts are some of the most prominent thoughts that you have, and they are the thoughts that drive your instinctual behaviors and habits. While you may not be aware of them, these unconscious thoughts have the power to most influence your actions and to dictate whether you are self-disciplined or not. Successful people know that before they can act the way that they want to that they have to learn to embrace their unconscious thoughts, but not only can the role of unconscious thoughts be seen through anecdotal evidence, but it can also be seen through research and neuroscience, so if you aren't convinced in the power of your unconscious mind yet, you will be.

When you can embrace your unconscious mind, you embrace important parts of yourself that people too often ignore because they are unaware of the power of their minds. They don't realize that all the thoughts that they don't think about are the ones that can make or break them. When trying to have self-discipline, most people focus on their conscious thoughts. They think, "Those thoughts I have about eating donuts are what kill me." The temptation isn't what destroys you. People can resist temptation. What destroys people are thoughts from the instinctual part of you that say, "Eat as many donuts as you can because, after this, I'm never allowing you to have any ever again." It is the all or nothing thinking that your unconscious mind promotes that makes it hard to stick to plans.

While the information in this chapter is scientific, don't worry, this chapter won't go too in-depth that you'll be overwhelmed, but it will give you a helpful understanding of how the brain works in a way that anyone can understand. People act based on all the things that have built up and informed us about our perspective of the world, but perspectives can be manipulated to suit our needs.

Why Your Unconscious Mind Matters

As you know, your unconscious thoughts do a lot for you. They are the reason that when a baseball comes flying at your face, you duck. They are the reason that you can drive to work in the morning without consciously thinking about which way you are going. They are the reason that you can so easily do things that you've done a million times before. Your unconscious mind is the source of all your habits, both the good and the bad, so how your unconscious mind is wired influences how you will behave. Thus, the key to self-discipline is this unconscious brain because it is your unconscious habits that usually dictate whether you will act in a disciplined way or not. You are easily able to have discipline over your conscious thoughts because you can rationally think through them, but your unconscious brain is harder to keep disciplined when you pay it no mind because it will cause you to act before you've taken the time to bring those thoughts into consciousness and determine if they are the right course for you to take. By making your unconscious thoughts conscious, you can change them, which is how habits are made and broken, a crucial step in self-discipline.

You cannot expect to make changes to your body, your professional life, or your outlook on life without addressing those unconscious thoughts. Research shows that the brain is like a muscle, so it can be trained the way you want it. Just like going to the gym and building muscles, it takes time and effort to build up the mental strength that will allow you to reach your goals. Your brain wants to do what is best for you. It wants to keep you safe and happy, but sometimes it misunderstands how to do that based on your habits, but by working out your brain muscles, you can show it new ways to satisfy you and keep you protected.

Through research, academics have realized just how important the stimuli around us are to our behavior. This stimulus is not something that we often are conscious of, but it feeds the unconscious parts of our brains with knowledge. It fuels our instincts in ways that we don't regularly notice. Gerald Zaltman, a Harvard professor, estimates that just five percent of our decisions are conscious. This unbalance between unconscious and conscious thoughts is foundational to how marketing works. You may want to tell yourself to stop buying sugary cereal, but doing that may be harder than you think because of your unconscious mind at work. You go to the store, you see the cereal, and suddenly, your resolve just disappears, and you put the cereal into our cart without much thought. Maybe you haven't eaten since lunch, and you're feeling ravenous, and your brain unconsciously brought up the commercial you saw for the cereal the night before as you ate dinner. Your brain is linked to being fed with that cereal, so it does not wonder that you gravitate towards it! The commercial was made to appeal to that part of your mind with its vibrancy and how delectable it looked. You could almost taste the cereal with how visceral the commercial was. Yet, it's not nutritionally helpful to you. It's filled with sugar and little else. It is exactly what you consciously didn't want.

With all that in mind, it can feel impossible to have self-discipline. You think that you'll never be able to counter the unconscious thoughts that drive you. You feel out of control of yourself. It feels like you're a victim of the stimuli around you, but that's not true. It is possible to take charge of your unconscious mind simply by fueling it with other information that counters the negative stimuli that you've been getting. You can take your unconscious thoughts, and in hindsight, you can bring them into the light and analyze them. With analysis, you can then resist those thoughts in the future. That is self-discipline. Self-discipline is that resolve to reshape the way you think and resist the expectations that you have for yourself and the world. It is ensuring that you never let yourself get too comfortable in your habits. It is living on the edge without the crippling anxiety that pushing your boundaries sometimes brings.

Daniel Kahneman's work in his book, *Thinking, Fast and Slow,* is a great source that shows the value of understanding your unconscious brain. In this groundbreaking book, he uses neuroscience to break the brain down into two systems, System 1 and System 2. These are the "fast" and the "slow" thinking, respectively. These parts of your brain work together to make decisions, and when they send the wrong messages to one another, that's when you start to make undisciplined decisions. Your brain becomes confused, and it is unable to remedy what you want with the other information that it has received in the past. Thus, it chooses the safe route that you've taken before because it views that as the best way to keep you safe. System 1 takes over because it is the animalistic part of you that wants to think quickly and avoid danger as soon as it feels threatened.

In its essence, System 1 is the instinctual part of you that is prone to snap judgments. Back in the olden days, when humans lived in the wild, any threat could mean life or death. Thus, humans learned to think quickly based on past experiences, so if a person had been attacked by a certain wild animal in the past, when they poked at it, they would know never to poke at it again. This can also be explained as your fight or flight system. That feeling that you get when you feel threatened or wanting to confront your problem or run away from it is System 1. You aren't conscious of the thought process that goes into System one. The decisions in this part of your brain are instantaneous. It's like seeing a math problem "one times one". You immediately know that the answer is one without having to think about it. Meanwhile, one hundred and four times one hundred and eighty will probably not be something that you instantly know. System 1 is always on high alert. It is ready to kick in at any moment because it is the part of your brain that you use the most, and it is also the part of your brain that allows you to access information without having to spend an exorbitant amount of time and energy.

System 2, meanwhile, is the lethargic part of your brain. It is known for its sloth. It doesn't want to be engaged when it doesn't have to because it takes more time and energy to use this part of your brain. If you're in the wild and you see a bear growling at you, you don't have time to analyze what you should do. You need to act right away, which is why System 1 would kick in during that situation. If you've ever felt yourself freeze in panic, you've felt the power System 1 has over you. System 2 is not the brain system that you want to use during an emergency, but when you need more rational and analytical answers, it is leaps and bounds better. It allows you to think through what you are doing using multiple inputs rather than just unconscious ones; however, System 2 takes the backseat whenever it can.

Even when you have time to think something through, System 2 won't want to work. When you're getting ready in the morning, System 1 will guide you. It will have you follow the same routine that you do every morning, even if that routine isn't optimal. Nevertheless, the routine saves you the energy it would take to always ask yourself, "Would it be better to brush my teeth before I get dressed or brush my teeth after I get dressed?" Imagine having to analyze every action you do. It would be dreadful. Habits, therefore, are like shortcuts. They allow you to do things more quickly and with less mental energy. Thus, good habits are like gold, and bad habits can ruin the progress of good habits.

The key to making better habits is consciousness. Through some effort and self-analysis, you can become aware of your unconscious thoughts, and when you become aware of them, you can change them. Use your System 1 and System 2 brains to your benefit rather than hating the way that your brain works. Your brain works in miraculous ways to keep you functioning and healthy. It strives to do what is best for you, and you can use your neuroscience to your advantage. The more you practice working with your brain rather than working against it, the more self-discipline that you will have.

There's also another part of your brain that makes a difference in how you behave. The Default Mode Network (DMN) was first studied by people like David Ingvar, who saw that this part of the brain became very active in resting people. Gusnard and Raichle then discovered that when people were active, this part of the brain had decreased activity. Thus, researchers concluded that this part of the brain was engaged when people were doing activities that didn't require extensive thought. They were later able to link this part of the brain to mental health issues like PTSD and depression. Further, overweight people tend to have higher levels of activity in the DMN. What this all means is that people who have more active DMN's can detract attention from what people are trying to focus on. It is anti-self-discipline. By addressing your unconscious thoughts, you can start decreasing the levels of activity in your DMN by channeling your focus and learning to reorient your thoughts while you're at rest. Techniques like meditation, hypnosis, and visualization can all help you lower your activity in the Default Mode Network, which can help you have better focus. There's still a lot to be learned about this part of the brain, but all that we do know does suggest how prominent it is in your actions and how self-disciplined that you can be.

Researchers have shown the importance of unconscious thoughts in decision-making through various studies. One of the most interesting studies is one where researchers had people choose hypothetical apartments. The participants were asked to choose the apartment that was their favorite instantly or with some time to unconsciously think it over. Whereas just under forty-percent of the instantaneous deciders chose the nicest apartment, sixty percent of the people who unconsciously pondered the apartments while they were distracted chose the best apartment.

Your unconscious brain has so much untapped power that you can channel simply by being aware of it. Of course, it takes time to master this part of your brain, but beginning now, you can make yourself aware of all the things that you commonly don't think about. You can take charge of your thoughts and teach yourself to think in ways that help you rather than hurt you. As you start to focus on your unconscious brain rather than your conscious one, you will quickly begin to see change. Clearly, unconscious thinking makes a difference without people even realizing it.

People Who Have Mastered Their Minds

Some of the most influential people in the world have used mental techniques like visualization to change their lives. They imagined who they wanted to be, and through that process, they were able to be self-disciplined and do what they needed to make their dreams come true. These people are not any better than other people. They do not merely have superior genes that have allowed them to be self-disciplined. Rather, they have trained their minds and become more attune with their unconscious thoughts, which has made all the difference. You can learn this same kind of mental discipline and have amazing results.

Many sports stars have started to address their mental game to become better at their sports. Lindsey Vonn, a skier, was able to become such a sensational skier because she learned to rely on her muscle memory and not get so worked up while she was racing. She was able to put her conscious fears aside to let her unconscious brain become attune with her instincts. Misty-May Trainor and Kerri Walsh are volleyball players who obtained Olympic gold medals and several other accolades through their ability to use visualization and imagine who they wanted to be in the future. They became self-disciplined by being able to take all that surrounded them and focus on the elements that allowed them to better their game. Russian Olympic teams commonly focus more of their energy on mental processes rather than just physical training. By doing this, they can beat the competition and use their skills to the fullest. In studies, it has been found that athletes who exert twenty-five percent of their time on mental preparation were less successful than those who exerted seventy-five percent. While physical training is important for athletes, it is their mindsets that set them apart from the rest. Mindset matters, and this is true in any profession or pursuit.

Another example of a person who has used their mind to become more successful is Oprah Winfrey. Oprah Winfrey came from immense poverty, but she went on to become one of the most influential women in the world as well as a self-made billionaire. Oprah spent her early years raised by her young, single mother, but she was sent to live with the man she grew to consider to be her father, Vernon Winfrey. While she was with him, she began working on the radio, and she worked her way through the ranks and was eventually able to start to get local news gigs. With work, she was able to have her own talk show, one of the most well-known of all time, and she currently has her own network (OWN). To obtain her success, Oprah has frequently used affirmations. She thinks that when you say something will come true that it does. Thus, saying that you will be successful tells your unconscious mind to bring that success to life, and then you end up having the success you dreamed of. When she was a child, feeling small and like there was little hope, she would remind herself that things would get better, and they did. While she has had other struggles in her adult life, such as with her weight, she has been able to conquer those problems too by continuing her mental affirmations. Through her unconscious mind, she was able to become one of the most successful people in the world.

Arnold Schwarzenegger and Will Smith are additional examples of actors who were able to conquer their circumstances through their mental processes. They were both able to resist people who doubted them by ensuring that they could make their dreams come true. They faced many obstacles, but they were able to remain self-disciplined by reaffirming their belief in themselves. They both came from humble beginnings, but their names live on and are still well-known today. Without their attunement to their unconscious thoughts, these men might not have been nearly as successful as they are. It's hard to get anywhere in life if you're stuck in the unconscious mindset that you are bound to fail.

You don't have to be a celebrity to use the power of your mind to your advantage. Your unconscious thoughts may not make you a billionaire, a celebrity, or a sports star, but they can help you achieve all the things that you've wanted to achieve. When you can master your unconscious mind, you open the door to experience that you never imagined that you could have. You are not limited by certain parts of your life. You are limited by yourself— your own brain. It's time to lift those limits and let yourself embrace the person who you want to be as well as the person you should be. It's time to not limit yourself anymore because you can assert your desire to change your life.

CHAPTER 19
Make The Choice To Change Your Life

Never Forget That You Are In Charge

You're the one who makes your journey, so never forget that you're always going to be the one deciding what to do. While your unconscious brain and other factors may make it feel like you have no autonomy over yourself, you always have autonomy over what you do. It takes effort to remain aware of yourself, but it's not an effort that is unmanageable. People just like you have proven that it is possible to be completely in control of your life and your outlook. Some things are out of your control, but when you master the things that are in your control, you'll have no problem managing any situation.

You aren't just in control of your actions. You are in charge of your identity. You can be whoever you decide. Your identity is yours to make. It doesn't matter who you were yesterday; you're allowed to define yourself; however, you want to today. If you want to be your own boss, be your own boss. Take on the attitude that a self-employed person would have and choose to act in a way that reflects who you want to be. In time, you'll start to become the thing that you want to be. Sometimes, it does help to fake it until you make it. Act the part even if you aren't it because that's the way to make your dreams a reality rather than keep them as perpetual fantasies.

There's no sense limiting yourself. Stop saying, "I want, but..." Limiting yourself isn't going to get you anywhere. You're not going to be able to do everything that you want, but by saying that you're limited, you're only going to further constrict yourself until you feel like you'll never do anything that you want. There's no bigger waste of time than telling yourself that you're stuck in a tiny, ugly box. Come on, you're better than that, and you'll be happier when you stop thinking that you're confined to a little space that doesn't give you satisfaction.

There's no point in trying to please others for validation. It's good when you can make other people happy, and there's nothing wrong with doing acts that make other people better, but you shouldn't use other people to define your success or what you want. Don't try to make other people happy at the expense of what you want. Don't be an accountant just because your mother always wanted you to become an accountant! Don't keep a toxic friend just because you promised that you would be friends forever when you were six. People are allowed to grow, and they are allowed to disappoint people sometimes. You can't please everyone, so you might as well please yourself.

Fate isn't going to try to stop you. When obstacles come, it isn't the universe trying to ruin your dream. It's just life. Obstacles happen, and it's not a sign that you're not meant to follow a dream. It's not an excuse to quit. It's a chance to keep going. Quitting will only make you have regrets, and it will prevent you from taking chances in the future. It can feel awful when you're sent off course and have to scramble to find your path again, but it really isn't the end of the world, and you can be resilient and come back from whatever problem you have.

Self-discipline means knowing that you're unstoppable. People who have self-discipline know that nothing can get them down. No matter what happens, they know that they are going to continue with their plan and fight for what they want. They aren't going to be stopped by anything or anyone that tries to stop them. Not everyone will want you to succeed, but as long as you have faith in yourself, nothing will stop you from finding success. You may have to go on a longer path, but you won't quit. You won't stop.

Don't Wait to Start

Tomorrow isn't going to wait for you. Tomorrows aren't going to stop coming just because you don't feel ready to make a change in your life. Those tomorrows are always going to come, and you'll find that they keep passing you over until you embrace today. Stop putting things off until tomorrow. It's a waste of time. You don't need a new day for a fresh start. You can have a fresh start right this very second, so stop making excuses about tomorrow and do what you need to do to be happier in your own skin.

There's never going to be a better time. It's tempting to fall into the mentality of waiting for a better time for a change. You think, "Maybe when the kids are grown," or "Maybe after I finish schooling," or "Maybe when I feel less tired." There are always going to be things that stand in your way and make it harder to accomplish what you want to, but while those things will change, they will never go away. There is never going to be an easier time to do what you want to do. You'll always have an excuse about why now isn't right. Now is right! You can make now work if you dedicate yourself to the present.

Stop hoping that someday things might be different. Just like you shouldn't wait for a better time to start, you shouldn't wait for the universe to intervene and automatically fix things for you. Things aren't going to get better if you don't put the time and effort in. Having a kid, getting married, graduating from college, or whatever other life even isn't going to be a fix-all. It's easy to think, "If I do this one thing, things will fall into place," but that's not how life works. It's not a carefully choreographed ballet in which everything happens as it should. Even in carefully choreographed ballets, sometimes mistakes are still made! Thus, you need to stop expecting everything to change at once and start making changes right now.

Make the changes that you need to make right this instant. That's the short answer to a huge problem. If you get to work right his second, you'll be victorious in whatever you try to do. Change isn't dependent on anything other than your will. If you want it to happen, it can. It's up to you how big of a role you take in determining how that change will impact you.

Work With Yourself

You are not your own enemy. There's no reason to vilify yourself. Don't act as though you are the evil force that you can never beat. You are in control of yourself, which means that you don't have to be someone you hate or an unruly miscreant within yourself. You are tamable, and you are in control of your mind, which means that you always have a say in how you will behave. Want to workout at the gym more? Workout at the gym more! That is the simple solution to the self-discipline problem—knowing that you can. You make choices every day, and those choices define your relationship with others and yourself.

Stop bullying yourself. You are not a punching bag for every problem in life. If a loved one gets sick from an illness, it is not your fault. Nevertheless, you can still find ways to blame yourself. You convince yourself that if you were a better person, then bad things wouldn't happen. You make yourself the reason for all the misery in the world. You are not a single person on a lonely Earth. There are billions of other people on this planet, and sometimes, the blame is no ones. Things happen, so don't beat yourself up over things that just occur. When you get sick, you'll have to miss a workout. That's not a sign that you lack discipline. It's merely something that happened.

Push yourself to be better. Always strive to be truer to yourself and to expect more. Do not expect yourself to be perfect, but expect that you will always have new goals to reach for. The second you stop reaching for goals is the moment when you know you've turned from the path of self-discipline.

Use your strengths and weaknesses to your advantage. Know your weaknesses and ameliorate them by using your strengths. Alternatively, turn your weaknesses into strengths. Maybe you have a temper. Use those feelings of anger and turn them into passion that you use for a project. No matter what strengths and weaknesses you have, you can use them in better ways.

Embrace everything that you are. Every little part of you can be added together to make yourself a better human. Don't be ashamed of who you are because that person is valuable. Your looks, your ideas, your dreams are all major parts of you that have worth. No one can take that worth away from you if you are content with who you are. If you feel ashamed about yourself, then you are running away from the identity that will give you self-discipline. You can't discipline yourself if you don't know yourself.

Self-discipline is in your hands. Having learned all the lessons in this book, you are now ready to take self-discipline into your own hands. It is up to you going forward to determine how you will treat yourself and the steps you will take to bring your aspirations to life. You have all the skills that you need to grow and become the version of yourself that is most ready to handle the challenges of the world. You don't have to give up on yourself. No matter what you want to do, you can persevere and push your limits. You can thrive. All you have to do is use yourself as an ally rather than an enemy.

Know that your success is up to you. This message has been reiterated throughout this book, but I am going to emphasize it one more time. You get to decide if you are successful. Your actions, your interactions with your unconscious brain, your beliefs in yourself will define your success. Keep repeating it until you believe it, "I define success."

CONCLUSION

In this book, you have learned the values of self-discipline, and I hope you feel motivated to have more autonomy over your life. Thank you for reading *Self-Discipline for Beginners,* and I hope that you can apply the lessons in this book to life so that you can accomplish your goals more easily and with more joy, than you've had when you accomplished goals in the past. Don't wait until tomorrow to apply these ideas. Incorporate them in your life right now, and embrace all that you have to offer the world.

To make the lessons in this book have an impact on your life, you need to practice them each day. You need to live boldly and strive to set yourself up for success. Every part of your life contributes to your self-discipline. The key to being disciplined is knowing yourself and believing yourself. If you have faith in yourself and tend to your needs, you will be able to conquer your life. You'll be able to reach your dreams with all the quitting and trying that normally comes with attempting goals.

An Amazon review is always loved if you found this book to be helpful. Feel free to share this information with loved ones in your life who could also benefit from learning how to be more self-disciplined. We could all use a little more practice in this area. Even people who are, for the most part, self-discipline have momentary lapses and need to reorient themselves using the tips and techniques in this book. Thanks again for reading. Go out and be disciplined!

DESCRIPTION

Self-Discipline for Beginners is a concise, understandable book that tells people how they can start embracing their true selves and establish self-discipline. Too many people feel lost within themselves. They are in a rut, and they feel uncertain that they will ever come out of that rut.

In a world that encourages instant gratification, many people want instantaneous results. They want to have rewards for their hard work right away. They want self-discipline, but it seems impossible to have that because of how much trouble people have following through with their goals. Most people don't even have clear goals! They wander through life, not sure about what they want or what they need to be self-disciplined about. They feel hopeless because they cannot seem to move forward. They spend their lives delaying their happiness. They wait for fate to step in and improve their circumstances.

If you've been spending your whole life trying to accomplish your goals but never completing anything that you started, you need to start reevaluating what is standing in your way. You need this book to help you understand why you lack the self-discipline that you need.

Maybe you too feel stuck. Maybe you feel like you've waited your whole life to accomplish certain things, but you aren't sure that you will ever fulfill your dreams because you don't know how to discipline yourself. You might feel like you don't have the personality to be as firm with yourself as you need to be, but you don't have to be as firm as you think. All it takes is some effort and a few simple steps to curate self-discipline. You don't need to be an authoritarian regime against yourself to have self-discipline. You don't need to run yourself weary or be of a certain personality type.

This book helps people clarify what they want, and it shows them how anyone can have self-disciplined. You don't need to have special genes. It urges you to stop waiting and to start embracing your own skills. Don't wait for fate to interfere because you'll wait forever to get what you want. Stop living life in the passenger's seat, and let yourself reach for your aspirations. Make goals and stick to them. Be the best person that you can possibly be. You can thrive, and by reading this book, you will be well on your way to becoming self-disciplined.

This book will teach you the following:
- What self-discipline is
- Why people are not self-disciplined
- How self-discipline helps you accomplish your goals
- Why you need to get to know yourself to have self-discipline
- How to accept the possibility of failure
- How to face the trauma that stands in your way
- Why you need to assert your worth to find your direction in life

- The importance of accepting criticism
- The value of making goals
- Why you should stop trying and start doing
- How positivity keeps you on track
- Why you need to embrace your unconscious mind to unlock your potential
- How to embrace changes to become self-disciplined today

MENTAL TOUGHNESS

Master Your Emotions, Develop Brain Strength With Cognitive Training Secrets, Control Your Thoughts and Feelings, Achieve the Self-Discipline to Succeed in Life

Lara Bennett

© Copyright 2020 by Lara Bennett. All right reserved.

The work contained herein has been produced with the intent to provide relevant knowledge and information on the topic on the topic described in the title for entertainment purposes only. While the author has gone to every extent to furnish up to date and true information, no claims can be made as to its accuracy or validity as the author has made no claims to be an expert on this topic. Notwithstanding, the reader is asked to do their own research and consult any subject matter experts they deem necessary to ensure the quality and accuracy of the material presented herein.

This statement is legally binding as deemed by the Committee of Publishers Association and the American Bar Association for the territory of the United States. Other jurisdictions may apply their own legal statutes. Any reproduction, transmission or copying of this material contained in this work without the express written consent of the copyright holder shall be deemed as a copyright violation as per the current legislation in force on the date of publishing and subsequent time thereafter. All additional works derived from this material may be claimed by the holder of this copyright.

The data, depictions, events, descriptions and all other information forthwith are considered to be true, fair and accurate unless the work is expressly described as a work of fiction. Regardless of the nature of this work, the Publisher is exempt from any responsibility of actions taken by the reader in conjunction with this work. The Publisher acknowledges that the reader acts of their own accord and releases the author and Publisher of any responsibility for the observance of tips, advice, counsel, strategies and techniques that may be offered in this volume.

INTRODUCTION

Congratulations on purchasing *Mental Toughness,* and thank you for doing so. In whatever environment we are in, our surroundings are filled with numerous triggers that can set us off at any time. These cues can be positive and set off emotions like joy, excitement, and happiness, or be negative and set off emotions like pain, sorrow, and anger. If these are not caused by our environment, then it can be from our internal thoughts. Whatever the case, these emotions are often instantaneous. They enter our minds before we even have a chance to process them, which leads to behavior that is seemingly unintended. As a result, most people feel helpless towards their emotions and believe there is nothing that can be done. For example, if someone or something makes them upset, it's that person or things fault.

What individuals need to start realizing is that it's completely on them what their emotions are. If someone makes them feel a certain way, that's because they allowed it. You may be wondering how this is possible since your feelings come about before you can even react. The truth is, even though our emotions come to us quickly, they are not impossible to manage. In fact, they are completely under our control and do not happen without our permission. We just need to learn how to be the boss of them, rather than them becoming the boss of us, which happens all too often.

Since people are not controlling their feelings appropriately, they lose control of their situations and their life, as a whole. This ultimately leads them down a path they would never consciously choose. No matter what you are planning to do, mismanaging your feelings will make you lose in the end because you will lose out on your desired objectives. Mastering your emotions allows you to handle issues with logic and reason. You will live with a rational mindset.

The following chapters will discuss the idea of mastering emotions and how to gain mental toughness. This is an essential skill to excel at if you want to gain the highest level of success in your life, in every aspect. It is the one thing you truly have control over, and if you give that up, you have lost whatever power you hold over your life. Beyond discussing mental toughness and its benefits, I will go over why people lose control of their lives, and action steps that anyone can take to gain that control back. No matter how deep you are, you can come back to the center. Finally, I will detail where your life can go with the power of mental toughness, including the idea of becoming an alpha, which is the ultimate example of being strong and independent.

Emotional intelligence is a subtopic that will also be discussed. The shortened version is known as EQ, and in many aspects, this is more critical than your IQ. It will have a great bearing on your success.

We, as people, do not realize how much our emotions dictate the directions we take every day. They can inspire us to keep moving towards the next step or cause us to backpedal from an action that had the potential to change our situation. It is impossible to know where our lives are headed and what the future truly holds, but once we have the ability to master our emotions, we can make better decisions that will improve our outcomes. We will make better decisions, which will lead to more meaningful actions. As you read through the different chapters, you will understand that emotional intelligence and mental toughness is something that can no longer be neglected or dismissed any longer. There are plenty of books on this subject on the market, thanks again for choosing this one! Every effort was made to ensure it is full of as much useful information as possible. Please enjoy!

CHAPTER 1
Control Your Emotions

"You own your feelings. You own your thoughts. You control both. No one has the right to any of it-to any of you without your permission."
-Carlos Wallace

You have probably experienced this many times in your life. You might have met up with someone, and they gave you a look or said something that you did not like. As a result, you became upset, sad, or even angry. Your first instinct is to blame the person or thing that made you feel this way. In some cases, you will let your frustrations out. For example, you will yell and scream at a person for saying hurtful things, or you will kick the couch because you ran into them, or you will lose your mind while doing an important task. Yes, you will place blame on anyone and everything that affects your emotions, except for the one person who deserves it the most, and that is you.

You are not going to want to hear this, but how you end up feeling in a situation is ultimately decided on by you, and nothing else. This means that you are the sole controller of your emotions and will decide how you react to whatever happens to you. While it's true that you cannot control the world, including other people, you can certainly manage yourself. Once you realize this, then your life will change in amazing ways. This is because you will take full responsibility for how things turn out. When you begin to think in this mindset, then you feel like you can accomplish your goals in every way.

Mastering your emotions does not mean you go through life without them. What it actually means is that they are purposeful, and you know the right moments to display them. When you do, you will get the reactions you want from other people. This will, in turn, lead to the outcomes you want, as well. As you read further, it will become apparent that your past was built by the emotions you displayed, and therefore, your future depends on how well you can manage them.

The Purpose of Emotions

Emotions serve a huge purpose for us. They plan an important role in how we think and behave. They motivate us to take action but can also make us fearful and retreat into our bunkers. For instance, when you wanted to pursue something, whether it was a goal or a new adventure, the steps you took were based on your emotions and how well you managed them. If you were pursuing a new career but were afraid, then you had two options: Give in to your fear and don't pursue any further, or overcome your fear and go for it, despite what the results might be. This is our life every day. We are constantly managing our emotions as we see fit, and those of us who can control them can use them to our advantage.

Emotions are meant to help us adapt. They provide us important information that helps us navigate every situation we are in. People relate emotions exclusively to how they feel, but they actually go much deeper than that. There are actually three separate ingredients that make up our emotions, and it is beneficial to understand all of these components to better understand your emotions. This will give you the basic foundational knowledge, which will make the tools and strategies used later on much more effective.

Ingredient #1: The Physical Component

This is the most obvious component of our emotions. It relates to how your body feels when you have certain emotions. This is why people state things like, "I feel happy" or "I feel angry." Sometimes, the feelings are distinct, but other times, they are so similar that it's hard to tell by these alone. This is why the physical component is an important aspect to consider, but not the most crucial one.

Ingredient #2: The Thinking Component

This is based on cognition and how a person interprets a situation. With the physical component, a person will feel something on the inside when their environment triggers them to some degree. With this particular component, you think about the event in a particular way, which can be based on many personal factors, and this leads to an emotional experience.

Ingredient #3: The Behavioral Component

This is the final component of emotion and what everyone can actually observe. If someone becomes angry, they will showcase it through certain actions, like yelling or throwing things. Many experts believe that our behaviors are separate from emotions and would not exist without the first two components. Basically, ingredients one and two lead to how we react. A particular situation leads to specific thoughts and physiological arousal, which results in our end behavior.

Understanding and recognizing these three components is the first step in being able to manage our emotions. Emotions can be short-lived or become enduring. They also serve certain purposes, which makes it even more imperative to learn why they exist. The following are some of the reasons we experience our unique feelings and the role they serve for us.

Emotions Can Motivate Action

Emotions can motivate us to act towards a certain task or goal. For example, if we have an exam to study for, the anxiety we feel over possibly failing it will lead us to prepare harder. If we have a sporting event that we need to get in shape for, then the fear of losing will inspire us in this case too. This is considering that we have control over our emotions. If we let the aforementioned anxiety and fear become too strong, then they can paralyze us to a certain degree.

People will also take certain actions so they can feel specific emotions, also.

For example, they might engage in a thrill-seeking activity to gain excitement.

Furthermore, activities that would create boredom or sadness might be avoided.

Emotions Help Us With Survival

Emotions are thought to be adaptive mechanisms that have allowed humans and animals to survive throughout the ages. For example, anger can cause us to be more courageous, so we can confront what is bothering us. Fear will cause us to retreat.

This can be seen with the fight-or-flight response. We can either stand and fight or run away and maintain safety. In both cases, certain physiological responses occur that cause us to react accordingly.

Other emotions, like love, can motivate us to seek out a mate and reproduce. Whatever our emotions may be, they can inspire us to act quickly to maximize our ability for survival and success.

Emotions Can Be Used for Making Decisions

The emotions we have can heavily influence the decisions we make. These decisions can be simple, like where to eat or what television show to watch, to more complicated ones, like which career path to take and who to marry. Emotions often play a huge role in what we decide, even if we're using a lot of logic and reasoning. For example, when we are choosing a career path, we may research things like job demand, pay, and opportunities for advancement. While all these factors will be considered, what will often be the deciding factor is how much we love the industry. Therefore, the impact of emotions on decision-making cannot be downplayed.

Emotions Help Connect People

When we communicate with people, there are subtle clues we can give off to help them understand us better. The emotions we portray through body language and facial expressions serve as cues for other people so they can get a sense of how we are feeling. They can determine if we are sad, happy, angry, fearful, or confused, so they decide the best way to approach us. Emotions can be expressed in words, too, especially if our nonverbal communication is not giving off the right hints.

Furthermore, we can recognize how other people are feeling by the cues they are giving off. We can interpret and react to emotions properly and decide what our friends, family, and others who are near us might need. This can be used protectively as well since we can determine if someone is angry and, therefore, approach them with caution. Also, we can recognize if we are upsetting someone by our behavior.

Overall, emotions can help connect people by having them understand their thoughts and feelings at any given moment. Valuing emotions, in this manner, can create healthy relationships.

As you can see, emotions play a major role in our everyday lives. They are not exclusive to the feelings we have but can also dictate the many different directions we may take.

The Idea of Controlling Your Emotions

Since our emotions can do so much for us, it is essential that we learn to control them, rather than them controlling us, which happens to many people. You have probably heard phrases like, "He could not control his tears," or "he was laughing uncontrollably. These terms denote that our emotions take us over sometimes and make us react in ways that we cannot control. In certain situations, we all lose control, and it usually is not a big deal when the moments are selective. For example, in extremely devastating situations, people will break down, which is understandable. Major issues arise when we are constantly at the mercy of our emotions on a continuous basis. When every action we take is reactionary to a feeling, then it's often not well thought out. In cases like these, the outcomes will not be favorable. Real-life examples of someone losing control include road rage incidents, acts of extreme violence, blowing up on someone for a minor incident, and many other words and actions that make us feel regret after the fact.

Emotions drive our thoughts and behaviors. Therefore, we must learn to manage them. Once we do, then we will be their masters. We will be able to guide them towards our benefit and use them strategically during various circumstances in our lives. Once we have a handle on our feelings, then we become mentally tough. To begin our journey, I will detail some effective strategies you can use to start having a hold of your emotions. After incorporating these into your life, you will understand that emotions do not occur without our volition.

Keep Your Body in Good Shape

A precursor to a happy emotional life is keeping a healthy physical body. There is a strong connection between what our body does, and the reaction we create through our emotions. This is also known as creating a healthy body budget, and there are many ways of making this happen. When you are in the moment, the simplest way to master your emotions is to get moving. For example, a simple walk through the neighborhood can decrease our neural activity and rumination, which is us focusing on distress, and thus improve our mental well-being.

Basic practices that are healthy include proper nutrition, exercise, and sleep are something you hear about all the time. There's a reason for that, and that's because they work. In addition, engaging in activities like yoga, meditation, or spending time in nature can do their part in increasing our body budget. Other simple practices you can incorporate into your life are showing gratitude, volunteering, and having positive social contacts. If you can include all of these strategies into your life, then you are well on your way to increasing and maintaining your body budget.

Gain New Concepts

You can gain new experiences in life through traveling, by reading new books, learning a new language, trying new foods, or watching different types of movies. Basically, engage in something that is unique to you and will help build up your perspective. This knowledge gains work by stimulating your brain so that you become more equipped at handling various situations. Also, it can increase your empathy for other people and improve your negotiating skills. As a result, instead of reacting harshly, you are more likely to handle something with calmness and poise.

Accept All of Your Emotions

A common mistake people make when trying to manage their emotions is to suppress or completely ignore them. That is not what mastering your emotions is all about. Suppressing your emotions only invalidates them, and your emotions are important to you, even if other people don't get them. There's a reason we should not tell people to calm down when they are going crazy. It makes them feel like they're not being listened to.

A better technique is to accept emotions as they come so you can get more comfortable with them. Comfort allows you to feel your emotions completely without reacting to them extremely. When you aren't' allowed to experience them, then you begin to lose control. Start thinking of emotions as messengers. Don't shoot the messenger because they are not good or evil. They are simply bringing you information. Use these emotions to learn about yourself and what you might be doing right or wrong. For example, if you are always becoming angry because you are losing your wallet, then recognize this fact and find a safe place to keep your wallet every time you put it down.

Assess the Impact of Your Emotions

Emotions that are allowed to regularly go out of control can affect many different areas of your life. It's important to set aside time so you can take stock of your uncontrolled emotions and the results they are creating for your everyday lives. Doing this will allow you to identify problem areas of your life and make the proper adjustments.

Keep a Mood Journal

Writing down your feelings and the responses they create is a good way to uncover some disruptive patterns in your life. Putting feelings onto paper can allow you to reflect on them. This also helps you determine specific circumstances that contribute to emotions that are harder to control. When you can identify triggers that set off your emotions, then you can come up with ways to manage them more productively. A good technique is to carry your journal around with you and write down intense emotions in real-time. Try to note the triggers that cause them too. For example, if you became angry, what made you feel that way suddenly. If the reaction you had did not help the situation, then use your journaling skills to come up with better solutions. Remember to make journaling a daily habit for the best results.

Take a Deep Breath
Deep breaths can be an effective real-time response when you feel your emotions going out of your control. This is true whether you are exceptionally happy or extremely angry. Deep breathing can calm your nerves in an instant. Taking slow and purposeful breaths will not make your emotions go away. That is not the point anyway. The objective is to slow yourself down and become grounded. This will remove you from the intensity of your feelings and prevent any extreme reactions. When you take a deep breath, do the following:
- Inhale slowly and make sure to use your diaphragm. You should be able to feel your breaths down to your abdomen.
- Hold your breath for about three seconds and then let it out slowly over one to two seconds.
- Some people will add in a positive mantra or statement as they're doing this. It's not necessary, but you can consider it.

Stay on Top of Stress
When you are overwhelmed with stress, then you will have a hard time with managing your emotions. This is even true for people who generally handle their emotions well. Reducing your stress levels will help your emotions become more manageable too. Some useful techniques to reduce your stress levels include:
- Getting plenty of sleep.
- Making the time to socialize with friends who you genuinely enjoy being around.
- Getting regular exercise.
- Spending time in nature by hiking, camping, or just taking a walk outside.
- Take the time to engage in hobbies you enjoy.

All of these techniques and strategies have to be practiced regularly. Once you gain a mastery of your emotions, then you are on your way to mental toughness. I will describe this in detail in the next section, and this will also be the underlying theme of this book.

Mental Toughness

Throughout any industry in life, we can separate out the winners from the losers. In the mainstream, this is most often seen in the world of sports, where there are clearly defined winners and losers. While talent and skill are necessary, they do not always determine who the winner is.

More often than not, they are defined by who was mentally tougher. In cases where two athletes were equal in their skill level, the one who showed extra grit is the one who usually the person who came out on top. The grit is what kept one person going when everyone else stopped. Mental toughness really comes into play when everything else fails, and all you have left is the determination and will to keep moving forward.

This is why there are so many unexpected victors in our society. These individuals were never given a chance because they weren't the smartest, strongest, or most talented, yet, they came out of nowhere and shocked everyone. They believed in themselves when nobody else did. Top performing athletes like Tom Brady and Michael Jordan have credited having a strong mindset for achieving some of their greatest victories. For example, in the Superbowl, where the New England Patriots beat the Seattle Seahawks, Brady made it clear that it was the team's mental toughness that led to a last-minute victory. Everyone thought the Patriots were done, except for the Patriots.

While sport's victories are the greatest example of mental toughness, it is not exclusive to this area. Being mentally tough is a strong attribute in any area of your life. If you are working out at the gym, it takes mental toughness to get through that last few minutes. If you are completing a difficult project for work, it takes mental toughness to keep pushing through, even though you want to give up. If you are trying to reach a goal, and there are many setbacks along the way, then mental toughness is what keeps you focused on your objective. Even if you want a happy marriage, you must have grit, because there will be many difficult moments that come up. In the end, you cannot succeed in the long run, if you are not tough mentally, because when all else fails, this will be the only thing that matters.

The Pillars of Mental Toughness

How you develop your mind will determine how well you perform in life. The great news is that mental toughness is not something you are born with and can be learned over time. You must develop and build numerous aspects of your personality to get to this point. Once you do, then you can accomplish anything. There are five pillars of mental toughness, and once you learn these skills, then you have the ability to succeed in life, and no one can stop you but yourself.

1. The first pillar is preparation. The more prepared you are in life, the better equipped you will be to handle what comes your way. Being prepared includes getting rid of distractions that will impede your outcomes. If you are an athlete, then you train, eat right, study techniques, and don't surround yourself with temptations. Whatever path you decide to pursue, the better your preparation, the fewer surprises you will have, and you will less likely be caught off guard. Of course, you cannot be prepared for

everything, and this is where the other pillars come into play. Here are a few points to consider for preparation.
   a. Are you doing your best to improve yourself every day?
   b. Do you know what your role is in your life and what is expected of you in certain settings, like in your home or office?
   c. Are you keeping up with all of your responsibilities?
   d. Are you ready for the potential for things to go bad?
   e. Are you adopting a positive attitude? Being positive allows you to handle situations much more prudently than being negative.
2. The second pillar is focus. Are you focused on your goals and the steps you need to achieve them? Get rid of as many distractions as you can so you are able to remain attentive towards the important things. Set up any reminders that you can to keep your mind on the prize. For example, if you have a career goal in mind, what are some things you can use to keep it in your mind? Perhaps mental or physical images of what having the job will feel like? If you maintain focus, then setbacks will not change your mind about what you want. Therefore, you will keep pushing forward until you achieve what you desire.
   a. Identify what is critical to your personal success.
   b. Keep a journal of your goals and update your progress constantly. This will help with your memory, too, as humans tend to forget things on a regular basis. Putting something down on paper also has a way of creating accountability.
   c. Maintain a balanced schedule. There is a misconception that you have to devote all of your time to a specific goal. The truth is, having a balance between the different areas of your life, like family, health, and social life will actually keep you from burning out.
3. The third pillar is controlling your arousal. This means keeping your nerves from getting overly excited or flat. This is called being in the zone, and it means you have just the right amount of arousal to get the job done. Too much arousal will make you overzealous and react excessively in certain situations, while too little arousal means you lack passion and motivation.
4. Confidence is the next pillar and don't think for one second that mental toughness can be achieved without confidence. Of course, confidence breeds success, and success breeds confidence, so if you can get into this cycle, then it's a winning formula. The key is to have confidence, even during setbacks. The following are a few strategies you can use to improve your confidence.

a. Goal setting: Set goals that you can control. They need to be specific and measurable. Set up a goal ladder with short-term, mid-term, and long-term goals. Take small steps each day to get closer to these goals and track your progress. Achievement, even in small form, can boost your confidence levels.
   b. Remain consistent and work hard. There are no shortcuts here. If you maintain a level of consistency, then you will make regular progress, which will raise your confidence.
   c. Positive self-talk is a great way to feel good about yourself. It is so easy to criticize ourselves, but we must change this to start speaking in a glowing manner. Ultimately, you will become what you tell yourself, so say good things, and you will boost your confidence.
5. The last pillar is resilience, which is the ability to handle stress, adversity, and failure. There are days when things just aren't going to be right, no matter how prepared, calm, focused, or confident you are. This is where the final pillar comes into play because you must not back down when things go wrong. If everyone did that, then there would never be any accomplishments in life. When adversity strikes, you can either run and hide or face it and overcome it.

I will go over various action steps to develop mental toughness in your life in later chapters. For now, understand that it is the trait that separates winners from losers more than anything else.

Habits of Mentally Tough People

> *"I have not failed. I've just found 10,000 ways that won't work."*
>
> -Thomas Edison

It is easy to see that mentally tough people live their lives in a different manner. Therefore, they also have different habits. Our mental toughness can be tested at any moment as we never know when a challenge will come about. Life is unpredictable, and those who are not ready to be tested, usually fall apart. Mentally tough individuals set themselves apart by seeing opportunities where others see obstacles. Going back to Thomas Edison, he once had his factory burn to the ground. Instead of complaining and giving up, he made an epic response:

> *"Thank goodness all our mistakes were burned up. Now we can start fresh."*
>
> -Thomas Edison

Mentally tough individuals have specific qualities and habits that make them who they are. These attributes are not only indicative of them having grit, but also increase their toughness even further. The following are certain habits you can begin developing now and will develop even more once you increase your mental capabilities.

Embrace Change

Mentally tough people understand the need to adapt and be flexible. The fear of change can be paralyzing, and it is not something these individuals contend with. Instead, they embrace change and even look for it because they know it will challenge them and help them grow. If you are closed off to change, then you will always have a dislike for it and will never see the positives. However, if you are open to change, then you will have more opportunity to capitalize on it. Mentally strong individuals are not afraid to leave their comfort zone.

They say "No"

"No" is a powerful word that needs to be spoken as a complete sentence. This means that you say "no" without any followup explanation. Mentally tough people have issues saying this word because they don't let other people's opinions bother them. They are too focused on improving themselves that they don't have time to care if someone is upset. Mentally tough people also don't use soft phrases like, "I'm not sure," or "I don't think I can." When they say "no," that's the final answer, and there's no negotiating after the fact.

They Neutralize Toxic People

It is difficult to deal with toxic people and sometimes unavoidable. A mentally tough person will not spend more time around a toxic person than they have to, but certain situations in life might warrant it. When they do need to deal with a toxic person, they approach them rationally. They do not allow negative emotions to fuel chaos and make situations worse. Basically, a mentally tough person will know how to deal with someone who is toxic if they have to.

Fear Does Not Control Them

A mentally tough person is not afraid to take risks. Fear does not control them. In the end, they realize they will regret the risks they did not take over the risks that ended up being failures.

They Embrace Failure

The road to success is paved with failure along the way, and if you have never failed at anything, then you have not tried enough things. Failure is a great way to learn what is not working for you, and mentally tough people use it as an opportunity to gain knowledge. Growth usually does not occur when you're happy, but when you're frustrated and ready to make some changes.

They Forgive, Even Without an Apology

Mentally tough people realize that holding grudges just makes their life more miserable. That's why they forgive people for doing them wrong, even if that individual is not sorry about it. It is the only way they can move on and live a smoother life. Forgiveness does not mean you condone the behavior. It simply means that you aren't a victim any longer.

They Don't Dwell on What They Can't Control
Life is unpredictable, and the world is full of catastrophic events. If you look long enough, you will see or hear something that will irritate you. The 24/7 bad news cycle does not help either. Mentally tough people do not get caught up in the bad news simply because they don't dwell on things they cannot control. If someone else is an evil human being, that is their choice. The mentally tough person knows he does not have to be this way.

Don't Let Opinions Rule Them
Once a mentally strong person has determined who they are and become proud of their accomplishments, they do not let the opinions of other people damage them. In essence, they do not care what other people think. In addition, they do not try to take the joy away from someone else. They don't judge others because they realize everyone has their own strengths and weaknesses.

Mental toughness is the foundation for success in anything you do in life. Once you master your emotions, you are on your way to becoming mentally tough. I will continue the discussion of mental toughness in the next chapter by describing a major component of it, which is emotional intelligence.

CHAPTER 2
Emotional Intelligence

Emotional intelligence is the ability to be aware of, control, and express one's emotions judiciously and with empathy. This is a major element of mental toughness, and without having this skill, you will have a difficult time managing anything in your life. It is considered more important than intelligence when it comes to succeeding in life because in the end, no matter how smart you are, if you cannot handle a situation appropriately, you will come out on the losing end. Many organizations have even found ways to test emotional intelligence before hiring someone because they feel it's a good indication of whether or not they will be a good leader or worker.

Of course, there is no scale or psychometric test that gives value to emotional intelligence, like there is for the intelligence quotient. For this reason, there has been criticism of the value this capability brings.

Having emotional intelligence means you are highly conscious of your emotions at any given moment, even the negative ones. In addition, you are in tune with the emotions of those around you, even if you are not interacting with them personally. Having this skill tends to make people better friends, parents, spouses, and leaders overall. When you possess this ability, you are aware of what is going on in your mind; therefore, you can better manage how you react to it. There is some purpose behind the actions you take, rather than behaving irrationally based on instant feelings. For example, if someone makes you mad, you do not automatically jump down their throats. You are able to recognize your anger and manage it appropriately with a more rational response. Furthermore, since you are able to understand the emotions of others, you will have more empathy and less judgment.

What Makes Up Emotional Intelligence?

You have probably met individuals in your life who always seem to be cool, calm, and collected. Despite what emotions may be going on inside of them, their outward demeanor never changes. They are able to handle the most awkward situations with grace and dignity. Also, people are attracted to them like magnets because of the aura that they give off. This does not happen by accident. This is emotional intelligence at its finest, and a select few individuals in the world possess high amounts of it. There are five specific components of emotional intelligence that make up the trait as a whole. I will introduce these separate elements and then go over how you can gauge your own emotional intelligence.

- Self-awareness: The ability to recognize and understand your emotions and the purpose they will serve. Self-awareness gives you the capability to understand your unique strengths and

- Self-regulation: This does not mean you suppress your emotions, but rather, you know the proper time and place to express them.
- Social skills: You have the ability to interact well and communicate with other people. This is because you understand what they are going through, as well.
- Empathy: Not only can you understand what someone is feeling, but you also have the ability to take on their emotions as your own as if you're literally walking in their shoes.
- Motivation: This is related to intrinsic motivation and not just what comes from external sources, like money or fame. Emotionally intelligent people have an internal passion that drives them.

Some people are born with emotional intelligence, while others develop it throughout their lives. Either way, it is an essential quality to have if you want to be mentally tough. The following are some signs of emotional intelligence.

- You have the ability to recognize emotions and the impact they will have on you and other people. As an emotionally intelligent person, you may find yourself asking the following questions.
    - What are my emotional strengths and weaknesses?
    - How will my current mood affect my thought and decision-making skills?
    - What are some of the reasons for what others are doing? What is the driving force behind their decisions?
- You take the time to pause before you speak or act on a situation. This is difficult for people who are reactionary, but once you have developed emotional intelligence, it will become natural for you. Taking a few extra seconds to think something over can save you a lifetime of grief. Pausing prevents permanent decision-making based on temporary emotions.
- You strive to control your thoughts based on the emotions that enter your mind.
- You do not become offended by criticism. Rather, you use it as a chance to learn. At the very least, it gives you a window into how other people think of you. When you receive constructive feedback, you will always ask how it can make you better. Keep in mind that there's a difference between constructive criticism and just being insulting.
- You show authenticity by saying what you mean and meaning what you say. It also means sticking to your principles above everything.

- You demonstrate empathy, which means you have a deep understanding of other people's thoughts and feelings. Instead of jumping to conclusions about others, you really try to understand them.
- You have no problem praising other people. Mentally weak people hate giving credit to others because they feel it reflects poorly on them. However, being emotionally intelligent gives you the confidence to give credit where it is due. People crave appreciation and will enjoy receiving it from you.
- You know how to be constructive in your feedback and avoid treating people harshly.
- You have the humility to apologize when necessary. Apologizing does not mean admitting you are wrong, but valuing personal relationships over ego.
- You have the ability to forgive, forget, and then move on. By forgiving, you no longer give the other party power over your feelings.
- You keep your commitments no matter how small they are. So many people make plans and then break them without a second thought. However, doing so creates trust issues. An emotionally intelligent person has a reputation for being reliable and trustworthy.
- You take the time to help other people, even if it's just a listening ear.

If you have any of these attributes, then there's a good chance you have some level of emotional intelligence. Since there is no numerical gauge in determining your level, you just have to do your best self-assessment. Of course, no matter how much emotional intelligence you have, there's room to build up more, which is what we will discuss in the next section.

Creating Emotional Intelligence

Now that I have gone over emotional intelligence, its value cannot be denied as an element of mental toughness. Emotional intelligence is a major driving force to success. I will now go over some action steps in developing this skill within yourself. As you increase your emotional intelligence, you will notice all areas of your life, including relationships, careers, and health, improving in ways you never imagined.

Reduce Negative Emotions

Managing our negative emotions is one of the most important aspects of gaining emotional intelligence. If we always think negatively, we will become overwhelmed by with these thoughts. There are two ways you can start shifting your thought patterns towards the positive.
- Avoid negative personalization: When someone is behaving in a poor manner, we have a tendency to jump to conclusions about

them. We automatically assume they are a bad person in some way. However, we need to stop assuming the worst and creating a negative caricature of the individual. Instead, try to come up with various reasons they might be acting in this manner. You might even come up with some nuclear examples. When we reduce negative personalization, then we can look at a person and a situation more objectively. When people are behaving in a strange manner, it is more of a reflection on them, rather than us. The point is, avoid thinking poorly about a person based on a single scenario.
- Reduce the fear of rejection: An effective way to manage your fear of rejection is to have multiple backup plans if one option fails. If you have strong alternatives to fall back on, it will quell your fear of being denied. Avoid putting all of your eggs into one basket. An example would be to apply for three or four jobs you are excited about, in addition to your dream job. Have high hopes that you will land your first choice, but if you don't, it won't be the end of the world because you will have other paths you can go down.

Stay Cool and Manage Stress

Everyone has various stressors in their lives, as they are unavoidable. How we handle stressful situations will ultimately determine what outcomes we create. When under extreme pressure, the last thing you want to do is blow a gasket, even though it can seem like the only option. Keeping cool in times of stress will create the best results for you. The following are some tips to help you remain calm and manage stress.
- When you're feeling nervous, try getting some cool, fresh air outside. Cool temperatures can reduce anxiety quickly. Another option is to splash cool water on your face. Please avoid anything that will stimulate the nervousness, like caffeine or sugar.
- If you are fearful, discouraged, or worn down, then try engaging in some exercise where you build up a sweat. The more you move and become active, the higher your confidence levels will grow. Whenever you feel down and out, get up, and do some fun physical activities.

Be Assertive and Express Difficult Emotions

You need to be able to set boundaries with people, so they know where they stand and recognize where your line is. To communicate this adequately, you need to be assertive. Assertiveness means you are respectful but firm in your statements. You are not meek in how you approach conversations. Also, assertiveness does not mean being accusatory or judgemental. This will put people on the defensive immediately. Simply state what you expect and remain grounded in your stance. The following are several tips on being assertive.

- Make proper eye contact. This does not mean you should stare or glare at someone. This can be off-putting, as well. Aim to maintain eye contact for at least 70% of the time. The person will appreciate this and feel respected.
- Maintain an upright and relaxed posture. You don't want to slouch, yet, you should avoid looking like a statue too.
- Be clear and concise with what you want. Be straightforward in your approach. There is no need to raise your voice. Simply speak in a normal tone, but just be direct. Do not make demands or try to be manipulative.
- Avoid dealing with a situation when you are frazzled. Take time out, do some deep breathing, go for a walk, and then return when you are more level-headed.
- Before engaging in an important conversation, do your research and make sure you have the right information.

Remain proactive and Not Reactive

You will interact with many unreasonable people throughout your life. If we are lucky, it is a chance encounter with a stranger, and we will never have to see that individual again. However, if it's someone we can't avoid dealing with, like a coworker, then more thorough measures need to take place. We can't control a challenging person, but we can certainly manage how they affect our mood and circumstances. The following are some ways to remain proactive, instead of reactive, when engaging with a difficult person.

- When you are upset or angry at someone, avoid yelling at them, or doing something else you will regret. Instead, take a deep breath and count to 10. In most cases, this will give you time to figure out a better way to handle a situation. If you are still upset after counting to 10, then step away if you can and revisit the issue later.
- You can use your empathy skills and try to put yourself in the other person's shoes. Consider what they might be dealing with at the moment. This is not done to excuse their behavior, but to remind you that it's an issue within themselves, and not you personally.

Develop Resiliency and the Ability to Bounce Back From Adversity

Life is not easy. You will have many setbacks and challenges. These are a given. What is not a given is how we act in relation to life's challenges. When you are faced with obstacles, do not just roll over and play the victim. Ask yourself what lessons you can learn. Develop some strategies for overcoming the obstacle by thinking outside the box. Life is not easy, but you can learn to bounce back from adversity.

Developing Self-Awareness

Self-awareness means you have a deep understanding of who you are as a person, including your personality traits, strengths, weaknesses, thoughts, beliefs, and values. When you develop this trait, you have the ability to understand other people and detect how they perceive you, as well. Self-awareness is often ignored because people do not want to look inward to see what may be lacking in their lives. If they did, then they could make some serious changes.

Becoming self-aware is an early action step in developing the life that you want. This is because you will have the capability to see where improvements need to be made and build a better life for yourself. Since self-awareness is the core component of emotional intelligence, I will go over some daily actions you can take to change your mindset towards being self-aware. These practices should be done daily until they become a habit for you. You can then start taking control of your situation.

Look at Yourself Objectively

People often have a distorted view of themselves. In some cases, they are extremely self-critical, while in others, they have an overblown ego. Very few are able to see themselves objectively like a third-party individual. When you look at yourself objectively, you can start accepting who you are, flaws and everything, and start making necessary improvements. To start assessing yourself in this manner, consider the following techniques.

- Write down what you think you are good at and what you need to improve on. Do not compare yourself to anyone else. Just focus on what makes you tick.
- Think about the accomplishments in your life that stand out to you. This is what you are proud of, and not what other people think you should be proud of.
- Think back on your childhood and try to remember what made you happy during those times. Do those same things make you happy now? What else in your life makes you happy, and what are the reasons for the changes?
- Take the opinions of other people in how they feel about you. Not because you want to change for them, but because you want more objective information about who you are. A great way to get this is by understanding how you are perceived.

Performing all of these tips will give you a brand new perspective on who you are. You may learn things you like and dislike, but the key is to improve where you can.

Keep a Journal

Recording your thoughts on paper is a great way to relieve your mind of ideas that you've been thinking about. These do not have to be related to a goal. They just have to be your genuine thoughts. Take time every night to write in your journal and use these moments to relive some of the major events of the day. This will help keep track of your day-to-day accomplishments and whether or not you're progressing each day. As you are writing things down, ask yourself if you're moving closer to your goals, if you are taking the time to help people, and if you're sticking to your values. You will be able to self-reflect and have a better idea of what you want out of life.

Write Down Your Goals, Plans, and Priorities

Write these things down in a different place from your journal entries. When you write down your goals and a plan to achieve them, they become more concrete. When you see your goals on paper, you will get an insight into who you are.

Perform Daily Self-Reflection

Self-reflection requires you to set aside time every day and do an honest assessment of yourself as a person. Commit to doing this practice daily to get a detailed perception of who you are and where you need to improve in your life. Ask yourself if you are living the life you imagined, and if not, then why? This exercise seems simple enough, but with the number of distractions we have in our lives, finding some quiet time is easier said than done. If you can, isolate yourself and don't bring anything with you that you don't need. If you need to go out into nature, then that works too. The bottom line is, find some time to do this daily, even if it's just for a few minutes.

Practice Mindfulness

Mindfulness is a powerful art with the objective of keeping you in the present moment. When this happens, you become more aware of your surroundings, along with your inner thoughts and feelings. We have a tendency to be focused on anything besides where we are at the current moment. With mindfulness, we notice our present circumstances more, so we can see what our life does and does not consist of.

Meditation is a common mindfulness practice. However, it is not the only one. Others include deep breathing exercises, yoga, going for a walk, or just sitting still and taking everything in. Whatever you can do to keep yourself in the present moment will put you in a state of mindfulness.

Developing the level of introspection needed for mindfulness is not easy, but certainly necessary if you want to gain a better understanding of who you are. Self-awareness will help you grow as a person, so do not dismiss any of these exercises.

I hope you found this whole chapter useful in regards to the benefits of emotional intelligence. Without this skill, you will lack mental toughness and fall short of creating the success you deserve in life. In the next chapter, I will delve further into the topic of mental toughness by describing the extreme benefits it carries.

CHAPTER 3
Benefits Of Being Mentally Tough

No matter where you are in your life and what you are doing, having a strong grasp of your emotions is imperative. If your thoughts and feelings go out of control, then your life will be in complete disarray. The focus of this chapter will be on all the benefits of mental toughness and how it can affect every area of our lives. Unfortunately, mental toughness is an often overlooked quality. In our schools, the curriculum teaches us specific subjects and critical thinking skills. At home, our parents teach us about discipline, having a good work ethic, or finding the right career. All of these are important and should not be ignored either, but without being mentally tough, you will never be able to handle the toughest situations in life. You will always retreat when the going gets tough, and as a result, you will never reach the next level in any area of your life. Mental toughness is what matters when everything else has failed.

Mental Toughness at Work

Most adults spend the majority of their waking hours at some sort of job. They will be faced with many challenges, like extra workload, difficult coworkers, tough managers, and even unruly customers, in some instances. When work becomes excruciating and pushes you to the limits, all of your training, knowledge, and policies might go right out the window. What will matter at this time is how mentally tough you are.

When you are exhausted from a long week, and you have to get up one more day to face the work hours, then you have to be mentally tough. If a customer is angry with you and nothing you have learned is working to quell their emotions, then mental toughness is what will get you through it once more. We cannot deny the importance of mental toughness in the workplace, regardless of what type of environment it is. No matter where you are, you will be challenged, either physically, mentally, emotionally, or all three.

Maintaining your mental toughness can be difficult, especially when you're being tested regularly with no end in sight. However, mental toughness is what separates the winners from the losers. The highest level earners in any industry achieved that status because of how much their minds can handle. For example, the salesperson for a company also reaches out to the greatest amount of clients. He probably gets told no more times than other salespeople even try. However, because he or she is willing to be consistent, despite being denied numerous times, they continue to succeed. When a client refuses their sale's pitch, they don't sit back and sulk. They accept the rejection and make the next call or meeting with confidence. Moving forward, despite failure, is one of the core values of mental toughness.

Employees of a company at any level, who are mentally tough, deliver more consistent results. They are able to stick to a schedule with much more discipline, whether they are motivated or not. If they know that something needs to get done, they will put in all of the efforts that they have at that moment. Mentally tough workers also have their priorities straight and will complete the most important tasks first. Most importantly, they do not run from their responsibilities, no matter how tough things get. Once they commit to something, they stay true to their word. If you work for a mentally tough person and they agree to work an extra shift or take on an additional project, you can bet that they will complete it.

When defining mental toughness in the world of sports, it can mean never missing a workout, training whether you are hurt or sick, and performing at your very best when the game is on the line. These same principles can be applied to the workplace, and some examples include:

- Arriving to work about 15 minutes early every day instead of arriving right on time because you hit the snooze alarm in the morning.
- Handing in your work ahead of schedule because you remained disciplined and did not procrastinate. Procrastination is a major productivity killer, and people practice it because they lack the mental toughness to work when they don't want to.
- Not calling in sick, unless there's literally no other option. Mentally tough people often don't want to show up to work, but they do anyway.
- Being calm and patient at the office, despite the constant chaos.

These practices will get you noticed. Whether or not you get daily recognition, your efforts cannot be denied by those who matter to you. This will lead to promotions, raises, and various other opportunities in the future. When you start applying mental toughness traits at work, you will find that you have a lighter mind, because you do not worry about things you cannot control. Also, you do not waste time judging or criticizing people. Instead, you give them credit for their achievements and are not threatened by them. All of this frees you up to focus on your own success. The great thing about winning is that it's contagious. This means that if other people see you performing well, it will inspire them to perform well too. Your personal attitude can go a long way in creating the work environment. Do your best to create a positive one.

Mental Toughness in Relationships

Imagine sitting at a restaurant and watching a couple at another table bickering over something. They are angry at each other, which is obvious to anyone who looks in their direction. The couple even starts shouting audibly at some point. These two individuals have obviously lost control of their emotions and cannot even manage them in a public setting. The couple in this scenario do not have the mental toughness to work well together. While it's certainly not fair to judge an entire relationship by one incident, the image being portrayed here is that of two people who are showing emotional weakness.

Mental toughness is imperative to have within relationships because two strong people will bring out the best in each other. This is because they challenge one another to be their best and support any goal efforts. They do not become jealous or envious when one person succeeds. They are happy for their partner and will celebrate with them every step of the way. Picture a person being upset when their spouse achieves a promotion at work. Actually, you don't have to imagine this because it happens all the time. Negative emotions like these create rifts within a relationship, and if things don't end, then the couple will be very unhappy together.

Mentally strong couples also practice healthy habits. These healthy habits are what continue to create strong bonds. While it's important to understand what strong couples do regularly, it is also important to recognize what they avoid. The following are some examples of what mentally strong couples don't do.

- They do not keep score. Wins and losses do not matter in a healthy relationship, as long as both members are winning together. They don't fight over petty stuff like whose turn it is to do the dishes or who forgot to put gas in the car. They are not concerned with who has done more or less, because they are partners in crime.
- Mentally strong couples do not compete. They don't compare career paths, income, who the kids like more, which one is better looking, or who is most responsible for the couple's success. They are a team, and if they do have enemies, it is not each other.
- They do not attack each other with insults or false accusations. They certainly do not fight or air their grievances in public. They may provide constructive feedback for improvement, but each partner takes responsibility for their thoughts, feelings, and actions.
- Mentally strong couples use healthy coping skills to deal with things like loneliness, anger, and sadness. One of these skills is having emotional intelligence. They also embrace discomfort when it is part of the healing process.
- They do not manipulate one another. Mentally strong couples practice assertive communication instead of the passive-aggressive style, so they always know where they stand. They speak openly about their concerns instead of holding things in and using them as ammo later on.
- Mentally strong couples are not perfect, and they know that. They will make many mistakes along the way, but the difference is, they

will apologize when they do and then forgive each other instead of holding onto a grudge.
- They don't take each other for granted. They know how blessed they are and will express gratitude regularly. They appreciate what their partners do for them and for who they are, in general.
- They don't minimize each others' feelings. Instead, they validate their partner's feelings, even if they seem outlandish for the situation. After this, they help them work through it, as needed.
- They do not spy on each other. While members of a relationship should not have anything to hide, it is not appropriate to snoop in your partner's personal belongings to try and get information.
- They do not speak ill of each other. Many couples like to get together with their friends and gossip about their mate's shortcomings. Both men and women do this, and it shows that the relationship is weak. Mentally strong couples do not bash each other to their friends but rather speak glowingly about them. Whatever issues they have are handled in a private setting. If they do express concerns about their relationship, it is because they want advice on solutions and are not trying to put their partners down in any way.
- They don't keep secrets from each other. This does not mean that they have to expose every issue about their past. However, they do not purposefully withhold information either. They especially do not hide things that could damage the relationship, like spending habits.
- They don't try to change each other. While a mentally strong couple will help each other grow and improve in certain ways, they do not try to change a person at their core. They love their partners for who they are. For example, if a husband likes to watch sports on Sunday, the wife will not try to stop him. Instead, she will either watch with him or find something else to do. Of course, I am not suggesting that the wife will also not be interested in sports.
- Mentally strong couples do not try to tame one another. They allow their partners the space to be themselves. This might mean that one individual will have to become involved in activities they are not particularly interested in.
- Mentally strong couples do not lose sight of their core values, no matter how busy life gets. These values may relate to work-ethic, social rules, relationship with family members, or personal spiritual beliefs.

As you can see, being mentally strong is essential to being in a healthy relationship. Without this trait, there will be no real love or trust for your partner. If the relationship does survive, it will rot with turmoil.

Mental Toughness in Personal Health

Getting our bodies physically fit is not an easy process. It takes a lot of time, effort, and persistence. There will be multiple failures along the way, and the mindset to overcome these failures is important. Physical health is also not limited to exercise. You must also eat right and practice many other healthy habits. All of this takes an extraordinary amount of discipline and mental toughness. Athletes who perform at the highest levels can do so because they have the mental capacity to make it through the most difficult training sessions, despite how they are feeling. My goal is not to turn you into a professional athlete, but the idea of becoming physically fit at any level requires you to be mentally tough.

First of all, the power of the mind plays a huge role in outcomes. A study by researcher Hendrik Mothes, of the University of Freiburg's Sports Medicine Department, found that if people simply believe that exercise will work, the effectiveness is much greater. When people would think positively, their behavior changed. They had higher spirits during their workout routines and would be more active with various exercises. The study included 76 men between the ages of 18-32. They all filled out a questionnaire asking about their mood and well-being. The subjects who reported more positive attitudes outperformed those who didn't. This study shines the light on the fact that the simple act of believing improves the end results.

Having a positive attitude will improve your personal fitness outcomes too. With that extra mental toughness, you will be able to do more with your workouts, which means the quality will improve. In addition, you will be willing to go that extra mile when you are tired, hurting, and just want to give up. Mental toughness will give you the strength to get up early and work out before going to work or spend an hour at the end of the day doing some physical exercises, despite being tired.

Finally, having mental toughness will make you more disciplined with other healthy habits. For example, instead of staying up late watching television or browsing social media, you will go to bed early, sleep soundly, and wake up refreshed the next morning. Also, instead of reaching for the donut, candy bar, or soda, you will choose a banana, smoothie, or water. Mental toughness gives you the power to choose healthier options over the desired options. So, the next time you want that chocolate pudding in the middle of the night, allow your mental toughness to veer you towards the Greek yogurt instead.

Mental Toughness and Achieving Goals

After all that we have said about mental toughness, it is easy to see how necessary it is when going after your goals. As you are going after your goals, there will be numerous roadblocks in the way. It does not matter what the goal is and what it's related to. In order to get past obstacles and achieve desired results, you need to have a high level of mental toughness. Without it, you will be lucky to get past setting the goal in the first place. The following are a few significant reasons why mental toughness is needed to be successful in obtaining your goals.

- Mental toughness conquers self-doubt. Whether you have ambitions to complete a triathlon or want to start a business, there will be times of great self-doubt. Even if it only happens occasionally, you will need to be mentally tough to overcome it. When you possess the mindset of a strong person, you can reframe your negative self-talk towards the positive and still go after your goals with confidence.
- Sticking to your goals is easy when you feel motivated, but what about those times you are not? There will be plenty of moments where you don't feel like working towards your goals, and if you give in every time, there will be a lot of missed opportunities. This is where mental toughness comes into play. When you have it, you will be able to dig deep inside of you to find the motivation you need.
- While going after your goals, you will be receiving a lot of advice, and much of it will not be sound or helpful. The feedback and opinions of other people can bring you down and deter you from your goals. Being mentally tough allows you to ignore unhelpful advice, stay true to your values, and keep you focused on making the best decisions for yourself. If you want advice, get it from people who have already been where you want to be.
- Hiding your mistakes or making excuses for them will ensure that you'll make them again. A mentally strong person does not hide their mistakes. They admit to them and then learn from them. They are not ashamed of the blunders in their lives because they realize they're another stepping stone to success.
- Mental toughness gives you courage, and you will need plenty of it when you are down and out with no end in sight. To obtain goals, you must leave your comfort zone, which means you might fall flat on your face. If you are mentally tough, this will not stop you.
- Mental toughness allows you to bounce back from failure because you are more resilient. You will have a high amount of self-worth that even repeated failures will not stop you.
- As you are going after your goals, there will be numerous emotions going through your mind. Being mentally tough allows you to regulate your feelings through emotional intelligence. This way, your judgments and decision-making skills will not become clouded.

There is not a single area in your life where mental toughness will not play a role at some point. Your overall lifestyle will improve when you

have the ability to keep your mind strong. The more you can do to increase your mental toughness, the better prepared you will be to handle life's problems. Consider a few more examples of mental toughness:
- A football player who is bruised, injured, and in a lot of pain, just scored the game-winning touchdown. The reason for this is his mental toughness.
- A surgeon is tired and in the middle of a serious operation. He is perspiring heavily and confused by what is going on. Things are not going as planned, but he has to get through the surgery because the patient's life depends on it. In the end, the procedure was a success because the surgeon showed mental toughness.
- A teacher is stressed out because her class is out of control, and she needs to teach them how to do proper math. She is about to lose it but maintains her composure. By the end of the class, she was able to complete the lesson, and several of the students learned something new, which was apparent by what they were able to regurgitate.

Now that I have detailed what mental toughness is and the multiple benefits that come from it, the next chapter will provide various action steps to increase your mental toughness.

CHAPTER 4
Action Steps To Become Mentally Tough

Now that we understand the advantages being mentally tough create for us in life, it is time to develop this skill within ourselves. Mental toughness is not something you are born with. It is developed through time. Some individuals became mentally tough because of the environment they were raised in, while others had to develop it themselves. The focus of this chapter will be to describe various action steps anyone can use to strengthen their mind and be ready to face any challenge that comes their way.

Developing mental toughness is about restructuring your mind to think in a different manner. Look at it from the standpoint of reconstructing a house. You will have to work in many different areas of the home, but in the end, your goal is to resurrect the building, so it looks better than before. This is the same concept to use when working on our minds. To make our minds more powerful, we have to restructure many different areas of it. Therefore, I will go over many different types of exercises that provide different benefits. In the end, all of these strategies will work together to increase your mental toughness. Even though we will discuss different strategies, you may notice some commonality as far as specific action steps.

Developing a Habit

Since the strategies I go over in this chapter need to become natural and done on a regular basis, I will use this first section to go over habits and how to develop them. You can use this information for the remainder of the exercises in this chapter. Habits are created over the long run through persistence. You cannot expect to change or develop a new one overnight. The following are specific action steps to build habits for success.

Make a Decision
Make a clear decision that you will begin acting in a certain manner 100% of the time. This can mean starting an exercise routine, eating better in the morning, or spending an hour everyday reading, etc. Make up your mind after doing your research and stick to it. Start performing the habit right away before changing your mind.

Do Not Allow Exceptions
Once you make a decision and commit to it, do not allow for exceptions in the early or formative stages of a habit pattern. For example, if you start running every morning, don't take a break after the third day. You will lose everything you worked for thus far. Stick to your new routine until it becomes automatic for you. In this case, once you are looking for

your running shoes as soon as you wake up, the routine has become natural.

Tell Other People
Inform others about your plans. Once you do this, it creates more accountability. When you feel like people are watching you, then you become much more disciplined and determined to succeed.

Visualize Yourself
See yourself performing your desired behavior in your mind's eye. For example, imagine yourself waking up every day and eating oatmeal with fruit rather than something overly greasy. The more often you visualize yourself performing your new habit, the quicker it will become part of your subconscious mind.

Create an Affirmation
This is a positive statement directed at your habit. Repeating an affirmation increases the speed at which you develop a new habit. If you plan on waking up by 6 AM every day, then repeatedly tell yourself, "I will wake up at 6 AM and get moving immediately."

Practice the Behavior Persistently
Practice your new behavior until it becomes automatic. Most experts believe that 21-days is the magic number for habit development. This is an average. To be safe, give yourself at least 30 days.

Reward Yourself
You deserve recognition for starting a habit pattern and following through on it. Find ways to reward yourself along the way.

Here are a few more steps to consider:
- Focus on one habit at a time. Trying to make too many changes at once can make you overwhelmed and cause confusion.
- Anchor your new habit to something you do anyway. For example, you can go to the gym after performing another errand that you generally do, like shopping or going to the bank. This will make it seem like less of an inconvenience.
- Take baby steps. Do not wake up on your first morning and try to run for an hour if you've never run before. Start with 10 minutes at a slow pace and build yourself up. Remain patient.
- Make whatever plans you can for possible obstacles. This will make you more prepared.

Good luck with forming your new habits with these different techniques.

Building Resilience

"It's not whether you get knocked down. It's whether you get up."
-Vince Lombardi

Resilience is your ability to bounce back after you have been knocked down, whether it's literally or figuratively. Everyone faces setbacks in life, no matter how talented, smart, or prepared they are. This is a given. But it does not matter how many setbacks you have. The important thing is that you can bounce back every time and keep moving forward. Think about the times in your life where you were knocked down. Were you quick to get up and keep moving? If not, then it's time to build up your mental resilience. Luckily, there are several practical steps you can start taking right away to build up this trait.

Our resilience is often tested when we are faced with unexpected circumstances like a job loss, death of a loved one, or a major injury. When these challenges occur, we have two options: Retreat and give up, or rise above and come back stronger than ever. It's true that you don't know how strong you really are until being strong is your only option. It is also true that no matter how much you build up your resiliency levels, life will still hit you with something that will stop you in your tracks. Nonetheless, the reason for becoming resilient is so you can be more prepared for life. The following are some effective strategies to get you started.

Skill Acquisition

You can build up your resilience by acquiring new skills. Learning a new skill set promotes a sense of mastery and competence. Both of these traits are useful during challenging times. Acquiring these new abilities will also improve your self-confidence and worth, which are also needed in order to be resilient. The skills you choose are personal. Just make sure they challenge you in some way. For example, if you are not great with manual dexterity, then take classes in woodworking or sculpting. If you are not light on your feet, take some dance classes. Whatever you are determined to learn, go out and do it.

Controlled Exposure

This refers to the gradual exposure to situations that provoke your anxiety. Doing this activity will slowly help you overcome your fears, so when you face them in the real world, they won't be such a big deal. Once again, the situations you choose will be personalized based on what fears you have. A common example is swimming. Many people are not good swimmers, and when they have the opportunity to do so, they avoid it like the plague. While swimming may not be an essential skill to have in everyday life, avoiding it all the time can become a nuisance for you. Instead, expose yourself slowly, depending on how much anxiety you have. For instance, go to a pool and dangle your feet in the water the first time. The next time, stand waist-deep. The third time, dunk your shoulders in. Go at your pace and comfort level; just create controlled exposure over time. When you are ready, start taking some swimming lessons. The main purpose of this is to put yourself in uncomfortable situations, so you are not in as much shock when they happen unexpectedly.

Make Positive Connections
Resilience can be strengthened when we create strong bonds with our family, friends, and community members who care about us. Having healthy relationships can offer a support system for us in times of distress. Likewise, being able to help others in their time of need can foster our own resiliency.

Stop Seeing Crises as Insurmountable Obstacles
We cannot change the events that happen around us, but we can manage how we react to them. When you are faced with a challenging situation, do not look at it as a large mountain that you cannot climb. Instead, break it down into smaller steps and then start taking action. Pretty soon, the issue will start getting resolved, and you will be much further along than when you started.

Take Decisive Actions
Take decisive actions whenever possible instead of shying away from a problem. Your problem will not go away on its own, so stop wishing that it does.

Keep Things in Perspective
There will always be tough times in life, but something to remember is that it can always get worse. Be appreciative that it isn't. Instead of blowing things out of proportion, keep in mind that everything eventually passes, and so will current hard times. Also, if you continue to build and work on yourself during difficult times, then the good times will be much more pleasant.

Look for Opportunities for Self-Discovery
Some of the greatest discoveries were made during the most downtrodden of times. People just had a vision that was related to the issues, and they came up with something spectacular. Or, they used their time in isolation to come up with the next great idea. For example, Uber was created in 2009 after the 2008 financial crisis. Many people have used difficult situations to take stock in their own lives and learn more about who they are. They may also work to improve themselves and develop a greater appreciation for life. Once you discover more about yourself, you truly learn what you're made of. You may also realize that you have already survived all of your best days, and you can survive the current circumstances, as well.

Maintain a Hopeful Outlook
If you are always expecting the worst things to happen, then you will have no hope for the future. As a result, your resiliency levels will go down. When you remain in a fearful state, you will be less likely to find a solution. Try maintaining an optimistic outlook instead. A great technique to help you with this is visualization, where you picture an end

result that is positive after overcoming obstacles and obtaining your desired goals. You can use physical images to help you with this too.

Learn from Your Past

A great way to be prepared for things in the future is to learn from your history. Think about your past and ask yourself how you reacted in challenging situations. Use some of the following questions to help guide you.

- What type of event was the most stressful for you?
- How did these particular events affect you?
- Were there important people in your life who helped you during these tough times?
- What did you learn about yourself and other people during times of distress?
- Was it helpful to assist others during difficult times?
- Were you able to overcome obstacles in the past that are similar to what you're going through now? If so, then how?
- What has helped you feel more hopeful about the future?

After going through all of these questions, not only will you learn more about yourself, but you will realize that you've already faced challenges that did not destroy you. You were able to overcome resistance before, and you can do it again.

When it comes to building resilience, there are different strategies that will be beneficial for different people. This means an approach that worked for one person will not necessarily work for someone else. That's okay. Find out what helps you and stick with those strategies.

Strategies to Embrace Change

The only constant in life is that change will occur, with or without our consent. The world around us is constantly transitioning, and we have two options: Deny it and get left behind, or embrace it and create our future. Everything is changing more rapidly than ever before, so we must become quick on our feet in regards to being adaptable. A big part of mental toughness is being flexible, and for this to occur, we must be ready to accept change in our lives and use it to our advantage. The following are some simple strategies you can employ to start embracing change effectively. Since we will have to deal with it anyway, why not make the best of it.

Keep a List

Start keeping a list of momentous changes in your life. With all that is happening in the world, it is difficult to remember all of the events we went through. Once we start recollecting them, we might realize that we have already been changing, and we survived through it. We might have even made our lives better. Make a list of the momentous occasions in your life, whether it was a new job, getting married, moving, having a child, or traveling someplace new. This can even be trying a new restaurant in town or taking a new route to get to work.

Find the time to jot these things down every day. Building up your list constantly and going back to reread it will remind you that you're changing all the time. You may not realize it, but it is happening. So, it should not be that scary anymore.

Look for Ways to Change

Instead of letting change happen to you, start happening to it. Actively seek to do things differently in your life instead of the same routine. Doing this adds change into your life slowly, plus makes things more enjoyable. Whatever type of change or new routine, you can come up with, engage in it. Just try to live a different life every day.

View Change as a Good Thing

Change does not have to be scary. In fact, it might be the greatest thing that happens to you. Start adopting the mindset that change is beneficial instead of something to be avoided. You can't avoid it even if you tried, so what's the point? Remind yourself always that change is a good thing. Even when things are going wrong, tell yourself that it's leading to something better later on. When you begin to see change in a positive light, there will be nuggets of good hidden even in the darkest situations.

Surround Yourself With the Right People

If you dislike change, it might be because you are surrounded by other people who feel the same way. Start changing your inner circle and incorporate people who are change-oriented. Eventually, you become like those you surround yourself with, so avoid those who want to stay in the same situation. That's for them, and it does not have to be for you. From now on, involve yourself with people who not only view change as good, but necessary for growth in life. Eventually, you will become excited about change too.

Feel Yourself Grow

Change allows you the opportunity to grow. In fact, it's impossible not to grow in some way. Unfortunately, this aspect is often overlooked as the growth that comes from subtle changes is not always noticeable. It's important to feel yourself grow with every new experience. Do regular assessments on yourself and your life and view the many ways you have changed towards the positive.

These are simple strategies that you can start using right away. Make sure to do them daily, so they become natural for you. Now that you understand how to embrace change, I will provide a quick list so you can recognize why you should do so.

- It allows you to learn new things that you might not have previously known or been exposed to. Even if the change involves failure, you will still learn.

- Accepting change makes you much more adaptable and flexible. You are able to deal with life much more easily.
- There will be many new chances and opportunities for success. This is not just related to a career. You will also have the chance to meet new people and try new things.
- Change leads to improvement. Improvement is not possible without change.
- If you remain stagnant, you can be good, but to become great, you must be ready for change.
- Embracing change reduces fear, which means you will become more courageous.
- Acceptance of change makes us more resilient and gives us grit. I feel like we've heard those words before.
- Change exposes your strengths. You realize what you are truly capable of, which you would not know if everything stayed the same.
- When you become used to change, you start to accept it, whether it's positive or negative.
- It makes you more proactive and puts the direction of your life in your own hands.
- Life becomes much more interesting and exciting. You will have many more stories to tell and experiences that you have lived.
- Experiencing change can make you more open-minded and empathetic towards others. This will eventually lead to better relationships.
- You are more likely to follow through on your ideas and reach your desired goals.

Practicing Mindfulness

Mindfulness is a natural quality that we all possess, and it is available to us at any moment. However, many of us don't practice it, either because we don't have time, don't know how, or don't even recognize it. Mindfulness is a mental state that is acquired by focusing one's awareness on the present moment. During this process, we are acknowledging and accepting our feelings, thoughts, and physical sensations. Basically, we are living in our present moment, rather than thinking or worrying about something else. The reason mindfulness is so important is that it's a great way to manage our emotions and build mental toughness. Once we achieve this state, the world and its triggers can no longer bother us, and we become fully in control of our thoughts and feelings.

The steps of mindfulness are simple, yet they are not easy. They require consistent effort and practice to become good. This means you must take the techniques of habit formation and apply them here. I will go over some effective ways to gain mindfulness in your daily life. You can practice these at various times, so take advantage whenever you have an opportunity.

Perform a Mindful Body Scan

A mindful body scan is a great way to get in touch with how you are feeling. With this technique, start from your toes and slowly move upward. As you do, focus on each area and assess how you feel. Notice any physical sensation or pain. This practice will make you heavily aware of what's going on with your own body. The purpose here is not to judge or come to a conclusion. It is simply to notice.

Practice Morning Breathing Exercises

When you get up each morning, practice focused breathing for about 10 minutes. Slow and deep breaths that follow a rhythm stimulates the parasympathetic nervous system, which is responsible for relaxing the body processes. This is why you will notice your heart rate and breathing rate go down, and also feel yourself become calmer.

Connect With Nature

This does not mean you have to go for a hike, even though it's a great activity. Just taking a few minutes each day to spend outside can have a profound effect on your physical and mental health. When you're walking to your car, going to the mailbox, or sitting in your backyard, stand there peacefully for a moment and feel your surroundings, whether it's the warmth from the sun, the cool breeze, or the smell of fresh-cut grass. Just notice and be present in your environment.

Notice Your Thoughts

Thoughts have a way of creeping into our minds, and before we know it, our minds become inundated with all sorts of negativity. If you allow your thoughts to run rampant, you will lose the ability to be creative. The worst time for this to happen is when you first wake up in the morning. This is the best time to come up with great ideas for the day.

A simple strategy to overcome this is to observe your thoughts by separating from them. Once you detach from your thoughts and feelings, you can look at them objectively and notice the effects they are having. This will allow you to remove some of the power they have over you.

Practice Transition Breathing:

Transition breathing is done in those moments where you are going from one activity to the other. For example, when you park your car and then run into work or wake up and jump on the computer. We often do these activities without allowing some time to decompress. Running from one place to another without taking a breather might seem like it's productive, but your work rate and capacity actually slow down. You become distracted and frazzled much more quickly. Taking the time to perform some deep breaths can calm your nerves and slow down your mind. This will allow you to tackle your next task with more clarity. This is what leads to real productivity.

Avoid Information Overload
Information overload can stress you out and overwhelm your mind. The beginning of your day sets the tone for the next several hours until you are ready to go to bed again. Instead of doing things like reading your email or getting on social media, try to read some inspirational passages. Use this content to educate you and challenge your way of thinking.

Visualize Your Daily Goals
Visualization is something we will frequently mention throughout this book because of the value it brings. Visualizing your daily goals can help to reduce anxiety, stress, and enhance your preparation. It will add more power to your physical and mental efforts. Visualizing requires mindfulness, focus, and creativity and will also free up your mind from mental chatter. As a result, you will see things more clearly.

Create a Coffee Ritual
Many people just stumble into their kitchen in the morning and make a cup of coffee or tea for themselves. They gulp it down, hopefully without burning their mouths, and then move on with their day. It can be beneficial to create a coffee ritual where you slow down while making a cup, inhaling the aroma, sitting down, and then savoring the flavor. This is not limited to coffee or tea. Whatever you like to drink in the mornings, use the same ritual.

Eat Breakfast Mindfully
Just like with their coffee, people inhale their breakfast without actually looking at what they eat. Also, take this time to slow down and enjoy your meal, which includes the preparation process. Enjoy every bite you take and allow it to satisfy your palate. Eating a healthy breakfast with mindfulness can set the stage for smart decisions for the remainder of the day.

Be Present With Your Family
When you are at work, think about work, when you are with family, leave work matters aside. Pay attention to your family members when it is their time. Learn about their day, what they are going through, any changes that have come about, and what people are planning for the future. If you don't do this, your family will grow apart and become strangers to you.

Practice Thinking Directed Towards an Outcome
Thinking is something we do throughout the day, and many of us tend to overthink. We end up thinking in ways that don't even make sense. Also, we often go through the motions in life, and our behavior has no real purpose. Instead of just going through life and performing tasks on autopilot, stop before you engage in anything, and practice your outcome-directed thinking and focus on your desired outcome for an

action you are taking. This will allow you to see more opportunities for success because you will actually be paying attention and thinking purposefully.

Stand, Stretch, and Move Around
If you have the kind of job where you sit around all day, then getting up and moving around is imperative. Be mindful of all the ways your body serves you and take care of it by standing, stretching, and moving to get the blood flow going. Stay in-tune with your body and what it's telling you. When you feel the aches and pains coming on, it's time to take a break.

Tune into Your Moods
People become so distracted at work and by living their daily lives that they completely ignore their moods. They may neglect oncoming stress, pain, anger, and other physical symptoms. Consciously acknowledging your moods can help you realize the impact they are having on you. Once you recognize this, you can work to change things.

Practice a Growth Mindset
People who have a fixed mindset believe that who they are and what they know is set in stone. As a result, they never grow and prosper. Instead, they just become stuck in their ways. With a growth mindset, you will know change is possible and necessary. Failures are not the end of the world, but a point from where you can grow. You become more willing to challenge yourself and accept calculated risks. Eventually, you will work for things you would have never thought of before and achieve in ways you never believed were capable of doing.

Practice a Shut Down Ritual
Mindfulness habits done at night can be a great way to help you fall asleep and rest peacefully through the night. Watching TV, playing on your phone, or other stimulating activities can have a detrimental impact on your sleep cycle. Roughly 30 minutes to an hour before bed, before mindful activities like deep breathing, stretching, meditation, or just sitting peacefully without noise. This will allow you to be in a state of calmness, so you can sleep easily during the night.

Never discount how much a good night of sleep will benefit you. It will allow you to start your day with greater mental and physical strength. So, put that device away and do something healthy with your mind.

Building Self-Confidence and Self-Esteem

A major part of being mentally tough is to keep pushing forward, even after failing time and again. There will be moments in your life where nothing seems to be going right, and this can be a huge shot to your confidence and self-esteem. However, these two attributes must be maintained because believing in yourself, and your skillset is imperative to being tough mentally.

Self-confidence and self-esteem are often used interchangeably; however, they technically mean something different. In a nutshell, self-confidence refers to how much faith you have in yourself in certain situations, while self-esteem relates to the overall value you place on yourself. As an example, you may see yourself as a valuable person, but lack confidence while performing a particular activity. I will break these two traits down individually and go over strategies to gain both of these in your life. Let's start with Self-esteem first.

Building Self-Esteem

Even through the roughest times of your life, you can still place a high value on yourself. This is what having self-esteem is all about. Once you raise your self-esteem, you will be happier, engage in less self-sabotaging behavior, and have improved relationships. The following are some of the most critical steps to help you start believing in yourself.

Silence Your Inner Critic

All of us have something on the inside that fills us up with doubt. It is a powerful voice, and it is known as your inner critic. It can put destructive thoughts in your head, like:
- You are too lazy and sloppy.
- You are not doing your job correctly, and you will eventually get exposed.
- You are not as attractive as your friends.
- Your spouse does not really love you.
- You do not bring the same value to the world as other people do.

While this voice can inspire you, and maybe even save you from a few things, it can also devastate your self-esteem levels. You don't have to accept any of this. You have simply been indoctrinated to do so since birth. It is now time to silence your inner critic and start changing how you view yourself. This can be easier said than done, but it still must be. One of the simplest techniques to do this is to literally tell your critic to stop when you hear it speaking. You may also use a similar word or phrase that has the same effect. For example, "Don't go there," or "That's enough out of you," can all be powerful in their own way. The goal is to silence that voice and halt it dead in its tracks.

After stopping your inner critic, work on refocusing your thoughts to be more constructive. For instance, if you were faced with an obstacle and told yourself it's impossible to overcome, tell that voice to be quiet and then shift your attention to action steps. Eventually, it will become easier to shut out your inner critic and remain focused on more productive matters.

Take a Short Appreciation Break

An appreciation break is when you pause for a few minutes each day and tell yourself the good qualities you possess. Do not tell me you have none because I know it's not true, no matter who you are. You can even do this multiple times throughout the day, as we have a tendency to be fixated on our negative aspects. There are plenty of toxic people who remind us, as well. I will tell you how to deal with them later.

To make this work, slow down and pause when you can. Now, ask yourself three or more things that you appreciate about who you are. It can be anything, and here are a few examples.

- I am always there for my friends when they need me.
- I always do nice things for my spouse on special occasions.
- I have never called in sick from work, no matter how I was feeling.
- **I wake up every morning and exercise.**

The list you make does not have to consist of anything major. It can be simple things that make up who you are. This practice of appreciation will not only build up your self-esteem in the long run but can actively alter your mood in real-time. Start doing this today and see how you begin to feel about yourself.

Taking this technique even further, before you go to bed every night, write down three things about yourself that you appreciate. That way, it will be the last thing you remember before going to be, and if you read the list after waking up, then it will be the first thing to start your day. Incorporate this with some of the mindfulness techniques from earlier, and you are well on your way to a tougher mindset.

At the end of every day, read everything that is on your list. You will learn that you have many great qualities after writing them down for several days.

Do the Right Thing

So the right thing every day. This is not just about morality. Doing the right thing can also refer to self-care, paying bills, or getting to work on time. When you know deep down that you're doing the right thing, it will make you feel good. It might not seem like it at the moment, but after the fact, you will not be questioning yourself. Doing the right thing is not easy, especially when it's harder and more strenuous, but the mental peace that follows will definitely be worth it.

Don't Aim for Perfectionism

Perfectionism is a killer of productivity. It can paralyze a person from taking action because they are so afraid of messing up. As a result, they procrastinate to the point that they have to rush or not get anything done at all. If you aim for perfectionism, you will lose in the long run, and your self-esteem will plummet.

The following are a few strategies to overcome procrastination.

- Go for "good enough." This is not a copout. If you try to make something perfect, it never will be. If you aim for "good enough,"

then you will be done more quickly. From here, you can work on making it better if you have time.
- Life will never be like you expect. Your day will not end with everything wrapped up as it does on a TV show. There will be things beyond your control, and focusing on fixing everything to perfection will just hurt you and your relationships in the long run.

Handle Mistakes in a More Positive Manner
Mistakes will happen throughout your life, and that's okay. Despite what you were led to believe growing up, making mistakes is acceptable and not the end of the world. The key to success is what happens after a mistake is made. People have a tendency to bash themselves repeatedly after messing up. However, you should not react this way. Be more positive in your approach by considering some of the following steps.
- Be your own best friend. Consider how you would treat a friend who makes a mistake and then treat yourself in the same manner. We are usually less critical with our friends, and it should not be this way.
- Find the upside to your mistake. Use it as a learning experience so you can correct it in the future.
- Praise yourself for making a mistake because you probably left your comfort zone, which is a great way to gain experience.

Be Kinder Towards Other People
Believe it or not, being mean to others does not make you feel better. In fact, this is a typical sign of having low self-esteem. People who place a high value on who they are don't go around being mean to people. Instead, start treating people with kindness, and you will not believe how much better you will feel.
When you show others kindness, the kindness reflects back on you too. First of all, people will treat you better, plus you will naturally be more kind to yourself. Whenever there is an opportunity to be nice, take it.

Try Something New
People often lower their value because they end up in a rut. Challenging yourself by going outside your comfort zone will make you feel better, even if you didn't perform the task well. At least you made an effort, which is more than a lot of people would do. This does not have to be anything huge. Just do something you've never done before.

Don't Compare
Falling into the comparison trap is a surefire way to lower your self-esteem because you will always fall short in some way. Instead, compare your current situation with where you used to be and see the progress that was made. If you are not satisfied, then continue to build and work harder. Remember, only compare yourself to your past and not other people, ever. Just focus on your own results.

Remember your "Why"

Your "why" is the reason that you want to do something, so remember what they are in regards to self-esteem. Always remember why you want to increase self-esteem and never lose track of those.

Surround Yourself with Supportive People

You might have to start changing your inner circle, but it will be worth it in the long run. Avoid highly critical people who simply want to judge and tear down people's dreams. Instead, spend your time around positive and uplifting people who support you. This includes your online and social media friends. Avoid those who you are constantly at odds with and join groups that are inspiring.

Building Self-Confidence

Now that I have covered self-esteem, our focus will be building up our self-confidence. Once again, self-confidence is having a belief in your abilities in various situations, so it's possible you will always lack it to some degree. The goal is to be ready to encounter as many of life's challenges as possible, and the more you push yourself, the greater your mental toughness grows. With each passing challenge, you are growing your ability to handle what the world has in store for you.

Self-confidence requires a lot of effort. It gets built over time with small successes. Some people look naturally more confident, but it's probably because of who they had around them. If you were not lucky in this regard, it's okay, because you still have time. Just be prepared to work hard and put in the repetition. If you want to build your confidence, start practicing the simple strategies below.

Present Yourself in a Confident Manner

Your appearance is a significant reflection of how you feel about yourself. Therefore, make yourself look good, and your confidence will show and grow. This is not exclusive to going to an event, like a party, or having a job interview. Whenever you go out, pay special attention to how you look. You don't have to wear a suit or fancy dress. Just wear clothes that you look good in and make you feel confident. This might mean nice jeans and a t-shirt. Do not ignore the footwear. Shoes are one of the first things that people notice about you.

This might sound like a weird trick, but it works. When you are at home, where no one can see you, and you have an important project, then wear nice clothes. This is a mind manipulation technique to boost your confidence, which will make you put in more effort into a project. Dressing better is not about impressing other people. When you look good, you feel good. If you catch a glimpse of yourself in the mirror and you are happy, that is a good sign.

Smile at People

Smiling at someone will not only make them like you more, but you will also feel happier, which improves your confidence levels. Smiling provides a more welcoming sensation. People are more at ease in your presence, and the quality of interactions improves. How often do you meet a salesperson who is not smiling?

A sincere smile, coupled with gentle eye contact, gives others the feeling that you're trustworthy. This type of behavior is assertive and benefits both parties.

Give Genuine Compliments

Giving people compliments is not only a sign of confidence, but it builds confidence too. The compliments should be genuine, and just like with finding appreciation in yourself, you can find real things to compliment in other people. Giving praise to other people will make you start seeing positive self-traits too. Eventually, this will build up your confidence levels. As a result, you will feel like you can handle more.

As you pass off kindness to other people, make sure to feel it within yourself. Doing this regularly will train your mind to start seeing positive things automatically. Get used to complimenting people you are close to and then move on to perfect strangers.

Appreciate the Good Things

This is similar to the practice we did for self-esteem, but instead of focusing on your personal traits, think about the good things you have in your life. The fact that you were able to acquire these items will help boost your confidence levels. Also, consider the past successes you have had in life and remember the fear you had at the time. If you were able to accomplish those things, then you can continue to do more in life.

Play to your Strengths

If there is a task that you cannot get right, and it is not necessary for you to complete, then leave it alone and focus on areas that you are geared towards your strengths. The more you perform the tasks that you are good at, the more your confidence will grow. You will continue to believe in your skillset.

Become okay with the fact that you will not excel at everything. Even the most seemingly perfect person you meet will not be good at everything. That's just the bottom line. If you have the opportunity to train more, then you can take it. However, you can also delegate the tasks you are not good at and keep your attention on the ones that you are.

Be Prepared

Being prepared in any way possible will allow you to be more ready for challenges that come up in the future. Preparation also includes practicing what you want to accomplish. For example, in sports, the players are going to practice their routines over and over again so they will execute them better when it's crunch time. In addition, they will keep themselves in tremendous shape. In whatever path you decide to go down in life, be as prepared as you can for the unknown, and you will walk around with more confidence.

Here is a simple scenario: When you have extra money in your bank account, you are much more prepared for emergencies that might happen. As a result, you are less stressed and more confident. Use the same approach for other areas of your life.

Set Goals and Work to Achieve Them
When you are wandering aimlessly with no purpose, you also lack confidence because you are not prepared for anything. However, if you set effective goals and work towards them, then your life has some direction. You know where you are going and how to get there. As you reach your goals, you will gain more confidence and can start setting bigger ones. With each success, you will gain another confidence notch.
A great way to maneuver here is by setting small goals. As you achieve them, you will gain more confidence. After a while, confidence will become the only thing you have. Be proud of every small achievement and use it for motivation.

Always Give your Best
There is an old adage that states, "If you are going to lose, then lose giving them your best." In this manner, you will have no regrets. Give the very best you have at the moment, no matter what activity you are engaging in. It will build into a habit, so if you are always giving lackluster effort, it will become natural for you. Eventually, you will start getting lazy with the important work too. Therefore, always give your best and walk away with pride knowing you did so. Make it a habit, so you create this mindset for every situation.
Remember this mantra: You are worthy of giving full effort into your goals and dreams. Respect yourself enough to recognize this.

Accept Disapproval
No matter what you decide to do in life, there will always be people who disapprove of it. However, you are not living to impress people. Your goal is to build the type of life you want. Therefore, you must learn to accept the disapproval and disappointment of other people. Once this happens, you will free up your mind and become your authentic self, not caring about what others think. The only person that you have to prove something to is yourself—no one else's opinion matters.
Approval seeking is a ravaging disease that takes away your happiness. Instead of worrying about your own needs, you become incessantly concerned with others. Think about it this way: People are judging you whether you realize it or not. When you realize this, it's time to stop caring, because the judgments will remain despite what changes occur. Eventually, seeking constant approval will strip you of your self-confidence.
Once you have built up your self-confidence and self-esteem, then you will have a much higher level of mental toughness, mainly because you will believe in yourself. Like all of the other exercises, these strategies must be practiced every day.

Avoiding Toxic People

I have touched on the idea of keeping positive people in your life, but I will cover it more in-depth in this section. Who you keep in your inner circle plays a huge role in your mental health, and ultimately, your toughness? Avoiding toxic people in your life as much as possible is essential. If you dislike dealing with someone and don't have to, then keep your distance from them. The following are some of the toxic people you should avoid completely in your life.

The One Who Love Gossip

If someone is willing to gossip to you, then they are willing to gossip about you. A person like this will just bring unnecessary drama into your life, and they are not to be trusted because you never know what they're doing behind the scenes to tear you down. It can seem enticing to peer into someone's personal life, but after a while, it will just become tiring and bring you no value whatsoever. It is just a waste of time to hear about the misfortunes of others, and you might not even know how truthful the gossip is. Eventually, it will just tear down your mood listening to so much negativity.

The Temperamental Person

This type of person has absolutely no control over their emotions and can go from astounding highs to devastating lows within minutes. This means they will lash out and project their feelings towards you constantly. They will even blame you for many of their problems, and this might make you feel guilty. As a result, it can be hard to dump these types of people, but it must be done. If you are constantly being used as an emotional dumping ground, it will weigh down heavily on your psyche. This needs to be avoided, no matter how difficult it is.

The Victim

The victim can be hard to identify because you will initially feel empathy for them. It can be hard to know at first, who is a perpetual victim and who is just going through a hard time. Eventually, it will become clear because the victim will need something all of the time. They can never get out of their bad luck and always fall back into the abyss of being a victim. Instead of seeing tough times as opportunities, they see them as suppression. This is the opposite of the person you want to be. The victim chooses to suffer all the time, and you will soon suffer repeatedly, too, if you do not remove them promptly from your life.

The Self-Absorbed

These individuals are completely in their own world and believe that everything revolves around them. After being around a self-absorbed person for a while, you will feel alone and isolated. You're merely there as a tool to help build their self-esteem and nothing else. Basically, it's a one-way relationship.

The Envious Person
Envious people always believe that other people's lives are greater than theirs. Even when something great happens to them, they get no satisfaction from it. They constantly measure their misfortunes against the world and even blame others for their lack of anything in life. Spending too much time around envious people can cause you to downplay all the great things in your life. You will also never be satisfied.

The Manipulator
Manipulators are the ones who pretend to be your friend but are actually just using you for your own benefits. They are extremely tactical in their approach, and if you are around them long enough, they will suck out all of your energy. These individuals can be difficult to figure out because they know what you like in every facet of life and will give you small bits of it before asking for something even more major in return. As a result, it becomes a one-sided relationship where you are giving up so much of your time and resource until you eventually become drained.

The Arrogant
Arrogant people will see everything you do as a personal challenge. They will never be happy for you, but just want to beat you. If you get a new job, it will be time for them to get a newer and better job. When you buy a big house, they will buy an even bigger house. Arrogant people will come off as confident, but it's really just a cover-up for their insecurities. They will always try to one-up you in every aspect, which will cause you to get burned out.

The Judgemental
Judgmental people will tell you everything that is wrong with your life, whether you ask them to or not. They feel that their opinion is of the highest validity and should be shared by everyone. Judgmental people definitely do not have a live-and-let-live mindset. Instead of being happy for someone who is living life their way, they feel the need to interject and tell them why they're wrong.

Basically, if you don't genuinely enjoy being around someone, they may not be a good fit for your life. If they are not necessary to you, then don't keep them. I am not telling you to use people; however, they should bring some value to your life, even if it's simple happiness.

How to Protect Yourself
Unfortunately, there are times when toxic individuals cannot be avoided. A common example is the workplace. The world is full of personalities who will drain your energy levels completely if you allow them to. People often don't recognize them or don't know how to deal with them. I went over some of the most common negative types in the previous section. Your best bet is to remove these people from your life and not deal with them at all. If that is not an option, then there are a few ways you can deal with these individuals, so they don't ruin your quality of life.

- Don't play into their reality. Toxic people pick out those who play their games. Don't get involved. Recognize what they are doing and get yourself away. For example, a perpetual victim might always blame someone else for their problems. Don't agree or reassure them of this. They might get upset, but who cares. They will probably start avoiding you because you aren't falling for their trap.
- A toxic person of any kind will do a lot of complaining. Do not join in and start complaining with them. Soon enough, you will become who you are.
- Identify how people make you feel in general. Sometimes, people are just having a bad day, and I certainly don't want you to judge them based on a single interaction. If they make you feel good most of the time, then they're probably a good person. But if you always feel negative around them, then it's a bad sign.
- Put yourself first. You can help someone who is struggling, however, not to the point that it destroys your own well-being.
- Be compassionate towards people, but don't try to fix them. They have to commit to changing themselves, and no one else can do it for them.
- Saying no to people and then walking away is not an easy thing to do. However, it must be done. When you do walk away, stick to your guns, and do not let up. The more you practice this, the better you will become at it.
- Always remember that you are not responsible for what other people are going through. Toxic people have a tendency to blame everyone else, including those helping them the most. It is a trick they use to get what they want. You don't have to fall for it. It is not your fault, so don't take the heat.
- Make yourself unavailable more often. If you are at a toxic person's beck-and-call all the time, then they will contact you at every moment. If you make yourself unavailable most of the time, they will lose interest and stop engaging with you as much.
- Do not spend more time around the toxic person than you have to. For example, if you work with them, then only deal with them for work matters. Don't meet at non-work hours and avoid engaging with them on personal topics while at work.
- Set boundaries with people. Boundaries will tell others what you will and will not tolerate. Communicate these boundaries with others and let them know when they have been crossed.
- Have an exit strategy for getting out of toxic conversations. People often don't want to leave conversations out of fear of being rude. However, you can dismiss yourself politely. Have some go-to lines, like, "Sorry, but I have to get back to my work."

The bottom line is if you have to spend time with someone who is toxic, do it in a way that won't negatively affect your life. Also, keep the association as succinct as possible. You decide how much you are willing to put up with, so don't tolerate a lot.

Being mentally tough is not about being a toxic person. In fact, it's about being the total opposite. The easiest way to avoid becoming toxic is to avoid those who are. The strategies above will help you do just that. Remember that you become who you surround yourself with. Therefore, build your inner circle to benefit you, and not someone else.

Increasing Energy

In order to have mental toughness, you need to save your energy levels. There is an old saying that fatigue will make cowards out of all of us. While it's true that mental toughness involves working through challenges, even fatigue, our bodies can still only take on so much. Maintaining adequate energy stores is imperative to success. The following are some tips you can incorporate into your life every day.

- Limit alcohol intake: This will allow you to sleep better and avoid morning grogginess. Plus, not drinking it during the day will help you avoid a mid-day slump.
- Use caffeine to your advantage. Caffeine can make you more alert and focused, but you must be strategic in how you drink it. Too much intake later in the day can affect your sleep patterns. Instead, reserve caffeine for the mornings and have a mid-morning one if you need a pick-me-up. Also, choose healthier caffeine options like green tea over soda.
- Drink plenty of water because proper hydration is essential for energy.
- Determine a proper sleep cycle. Remember that oversleeping is not good. You might have noticed that you feel more tired after oversleeping. Instead, try sleeping for just four hours one night, and then increase from there until you feel like you have had enough sleep. On the same note, if you wake up before your alarm and feel refreshed, then get out of bed and avoid going back to sleep. If you feel refreshed, then you have gotten enough sleep.
- Eat a healthier diet with nutrient-dense foods that include whole grains, fruits, vegetables, lean meats, poultry, nuts, and healthy oils, like olive oil. Avoid foods with excess sugar or saturated fats.
- Exercise regularly, even if it's just a brisk walk.
- Lighten your load for the day. You don't have to say yes to everything, and if you want to avoid social interactions, then do so.

Maintain your energy levels throughout the day, and you will be in fighting shape.

I hope you enjoyed these various strategies for becoming a mentally tough person. I know there are many, but reconstructing your mindset takes a lot of effort, and you must attack this project from multiple angles. In the next chapter, I will briefly discuss incorporating these strategies into your life.

CHAPTER 5
Practicing Mental Toughness At Your Own Pace

In the previous chapter, I discussed numerous exercises for building up your mental toughness. Of course, if you do nothing with the information, it is ultimately useless. Information without a plan is disorganized, and a plan without action will get you nowhere. The focus of this chapter will be developing a unique plan for mental toughness and then executing it in real life. Since the average time for developing a habit is roughly 21-days, we will set up a four-week plan to get you more mentally tough. This will be more of a transition period schedule.

Remember that the objective here is to build up a routine to the point where it becomes natural. Soon enough, you will simply wake up and start performing tasks without any triggers. What is presented here is just a sample routine. You can create your own as you see fit, depending on your schedule and various other factors. The objective is to build mental toughness through practice. So, let's start practicing.

Four-Week Plan

Week 1: The Starting Off Point

On week one, we will slowly start incorporating small changes and build on them over time. You will not make a complete overhaul immediately, nor do I want you to. This must become a natural process which makes the transition feel more seamless

Sunday: For Sunday morning, set your alarm clock for about 15 minutes earlier than usual, and when it goes off, jump out of bed right away. The first thing you should do is drink a glass of water to get hydrated and perform a mindfulness practice for at least one to two minutes. One of the best strategies is to stand still and take some deep breaths. This will be day one and a great way to get your morning started. For the remainder of the day, drink a lot of water to keep up your hydration. This step is essential.

Monday: For Monday morning, set your alarm clock to go off 15 minutes earlier than the day before and then just out of bed right away. Lying in bed is just a waste of time and will make you less productive for the remainder of the day. As soon as you wake up, drink a glass of water, and practice some mindfulness techniques. Perform these for a few extra minutes longer than before. While you shower, take some more time to practice mindfulness. While you are at work, start assessing some of your coworkers and determine which of them are toxic to you. Figure out whether you have been spending unnecessary time with them.

Tuesday: Wake up another 15 minutes earlier than you did on Monday. Determine what your ultimate wakeup time will be and keep getting up earlier until you reach that goal. Also, practice going to bed earlier the night before so you can still get a decent amount of sleep. After drinking your water and practicing mindfulness, get a good exercise routine going. This can just be a quick 15 minutes of stretching, lifting some weights, jogging in place, or whatever you want to do to get your heart pumping. Consider any physical or health limitations. While at work, continue to recognize the toxic people and start practicing avoidance, or keeping your distance. Even if you can cut down your interactions by just a few minutes, that is still some progress that you can build on.

Wednesday: For our fourth day, repeat the same morning routine and wake up an extra 15 minutes earlier than before. Increase your time practicing mindfulness and exercising. As you get more comfortable with mindfulness, begin doing it for other settings, like when you're driving, or before you start something major. While at your job, I want you to practice more on keeping toxic people at bay. Start making your conversations more succinct, avoid getting caught up in the unnecessary drama, and don't spend more time with these individuals than you have to. On this day, start focusing more on your work and less on what other people are doing.

Thursday: For Thursday, we will start challenging ourselves. In addition to the action steps, I have gone over, do something today that really challenges you physically, mentally, or both. This can be anything from starting a new physical routine, learning a new skill, taking on a difficult project at work, or reading a new type of book. The goal is to challenge yourself as much as possible.

Friday: On this day, do what you've already been doing and also develop some type of nighttime ritual. This should include going to bed at an earlier hour, eating healthier meals, and ignoring any negative news. This is why you stay off social media and don't watch television 30 minutes before going to bed. Instead, read a book, meditate, take a bath, or just sit down and relax.

Saturday: Put everything together on this day. Perform your routine in the morning of getting up early, drinking water, exercising, and getting ready for work. Throughout the remainder of the day, avoid or maintain distance from toxic people, perform activities that challenge yourself, drink plenty of water, and eat healthier meals. Practice your nighttime ritual and fall asleep soundly.

Week 2 and Beyond

Not that you have developed a full routine the first week. Spend the remainder of the three weeks living your life in this manner. Do not take any breaks because I want you to fulfill the entire 21-day cycle. After that, you will have been indoctrinated with your new lifestyle and mindset. Once the 21-days are over, you will continue to live your life in your new way because it will be natural for you. As you go along with the three

weeks, add additional steps to improve your mindset and toughness. The following are the key concepts to be aware of during the 21 days.
- Practice mindfulness techniques throughout the day.
- Maintain your boundaries and stand up for yourself.
- Self-care is essential, and should never take a backseat.
- Challenge yourself every day with something new.
- Work hard and remain focused on the task at hand.
- Eat a healthy diet and exercise regularly.
- When you experience pushback, do not retreat, no matter how difficult it gets.

Good luck with your 4-week plan.

The Power of Replacement

Through all of the techniques and strategies, I went over in the previous chapter, a common theme throughout all of them is replacement. Basically, you are replacing negative behaviors for positive ones. Once you start doing this regularly, the replacements will become the new normal. Here is a quick rundown of how this can work:

- Replace negative and toxic friends with mentors.
- Replace time-wasting activities like watching television with reading or learning new activities. Imagine if you spent an hour learning a new skill rather than watching a movie on Netflix. Your mind would become much sharper.
- Replace unhealthy drinks like soda or alcohol with water and fresh juices.
- Replace gossip with meaningful conversations. Meaningful conversations are where you learn something. Gossiping incessantly is just being petty and brings no value to your life.
- Replace complaining with having gratitude.
- Replace weekend plans with life plans.
- Replace worrying about the future with living in the present moment.
- Replace thinking about your next vacation with thinking about your next move.

I am not saying you can ever have fun or relax. That is an important part of life too. However, we get caught up in behavior that does not move our life forward and build up our strength, so we must replace those actions with more quality ones.

Mental Toughness Daily Tricks

If you want to become a success, then you must do what successful people do every day. Successful people act with mental toughness, no matter what they are going through. I have gone over several action steps and strategies already to build up mental toughness. In this section, I will give a rundown of what you can do daily to maintain your strong mindset.

- Act like you are always in control of everything. The truth is that you absolutely are. You cannot control what happens around you, but you can control how you respond. For this to occur, do not worry about what you have no power over. Worry about how you will handle things that happen to you.
- On the same note, put aside things you cannot impact. Or do what you can do and then leave the rest up to fate. For example, if you are worried about who a political candidate will be, then do your part in helping a person get elected. This includes holding fundraisers, getting the word out, and then going out and voting. The rest is out of your hands and does not need your attention.
- Learn from your past and then move on. The past was a training exercise for all of the big games ahead. Excessively thinking about what you have done will just set you back.
- Celebrate the success of other people. Resentment sucks up a massive amount of mental energy, and you will lose focus on what matters, which is your ultimate goal. When someone does well in life, congratulate them and then move on.
- Your words have excessive power over you. Treat them well. Instead of whining and complaining every day, put your efforts into coming up with a solution.
- Focus on impressing yourself, and no one else. When you wake up in the morning, consider what clothes will make you feel good, and don't worry about anyone else.
- In the morning and at night, plus anytime that you can in between, count your blessings. They will give you strength and inspiration.

Once you start living your daily life in this manner, your attitude will change in immense ways. You will start living as a mentally tough person no matter what path in life you choose. Mental toughness does not discriminate. It comes to those who practice it.

CHAPTER 6
Becoming An Alpha

One of the results of increasing your mental toughness is becoming an alpha in your life. The term is often associated with males, but it can relate to anyone who carries the personality traits. There are plenty of women who are powerful, tough, take charge of their lives, and don't answer to anyone. That is what being an alpha is all about. Unfortunately, there are many misconceptions about this personality type, which gives it a negative image in society. The focus of this chapter will be to describe the true alpha characteristics, the benefits it brings to your life, and the many myths that come with it. By the end, you will understand that being an alpha is a good thing and will never want to be anything else.

The Alpha Characteristics

The alpha personality refers to a person who is highly driven, independent, and strong. They are usually the leaders of a pack, not because they were assigned to it, but because their personalities demanded it. The term is most often associated with men due to stereotypes that exist; however, both sexes can possess the qualities of a true alpha, who are the strongest people in our society. These are the individuals who make important decisions, run the biggest companies, have ownership of their life, and have complete control over their emotions. Most of all, they are mentally tough and don't allow life's obstacles to bring them down. Every walk of life has alphas in them as they are found at the top of the heap in any setting. You can't keep an alpha down because as the expression goes, the cream always rises to the top.

While there are many types of alphas in our world, they all share some foundational characteristics. Once you increase your mental toughness levels, you will start noticing these traits matriculating into your life. The following are some important things that alphas do every day. If you do these already, then you might already have some alpha qualities.

- Alphas love being alone. Many people believe that being alpha means you are the most outgoing person there is. Truthfully, alphas love being alone. It is their time to unwind and recharge themselves. They get to focus on themselves and do the things they love. Being an alpha is not easy, so alone time is necessary.
- They say what is on their mind and don't hold back. If something needs to be said, they are more interested in getting the information out than they are with sparing hurt feelings. This does not mean they are not compassionate, but they feel honesty is more important than sugar coating.

- They don't care what other people think of them. Alphas know who they are and place a high value themselves, so other people's opinions do not matter. While they might take advice when needed, they make the ultimate call and don't allow anyone else to dominate their opinions.
- They care more about actions than words. While many people talk about what they'll do, alphas are actually out there doing it. Also, they stick to their word. If an alpha says they will do something, rest assured they will do it. People who do not keep their commitments are not liked well by an alpha. They can't comprehend why someone would not do what they said they would.
- Alphas are highly protective of themselves and the people they care about. One thing that will make them lose their cool is when someone is trying to take something that belongs to them.
- They are very passionate about everything they do. It gets to the point that everyone else needs to become as passionate as they are. This can make the alpha come off as bossy, but they are really just trying to get things done.
- They have strong beliefs in every aspect of their life, and it will take a lot for them to change. They also stand by their beliefs and live true to their values no matter the criticism they receive.
- They can be workaholics and love taking on extra responsibility.
- They only do the things they love and do not waste time with activities that don't bring them joy.
- While they are kind and courteous, they will not pretend to like someone they don't.
- They are obsessive learners. Any opportunity they have to learn something new, they take it.
- They have a high level of emotional intelligence, which allows them to manage their emotions in almost any setting.
- They care about their appearance, not because of what other people think, but because of their own pride.

Alphas have strong personalities and are often filled with charisma. Their personality attracts people, which also makes them great leaders. Alphas can be divided further into categories based on their specific strengths. In whatever style that is in question, the alpha will bring their own level of intensity, energy, and competitiveness to the table. Here is a breakdown of four different alpha types.

- The Commander: These individuals are intense and magnetic leaders who set the tone for whatever environment they are in. This can be a literal battlefield or a busy office environment.
- The Visionaries: These people are intuitive, proactive, and future-oriented. They see opportunities that others will dismiss, which

makes them very creative at problem-solving. They have the ability to inspire others with their vision.
- Strategists: The name says it all. Strategists care about strategy. They are systematic in their approach and based their decisions on data and facts. Strategists have a sharp eye for patterns and problems.
- Executors: The last type of alphas are tireless, goal-oriented doers who push plans forward and always have the end result in mind. They will overcome all obstacles by any means necessary and will push other people to do the same.

As you can see, alphas are not the type of people to be trifled with. They can be your best friend or your worst enemy. However, the worst thing you can do is get in their way. They are on a mission in life and will not slow down for anybody. If you can't keep up with them, then at least stay out of their way.

Benefits of Becoming an Alpha

Your alpha personality will bring you a lot of success in life. There is a reason why some people succeed over and over again, and it is not related to luck. While luck can play a part, there is no denying that the harder you work, the luckier you get. Alphas, whether they are male or female, show distinct qualities about them that make them winners in every aspect. They don't accept defeat and will never let obstacles keep them down. They will find a way to earn their goals, no matter how long it takes. In this section, I will focus on the benefits of becoming an alpha to get you more excited about gaining mental toughness. Remember that it all starts from there.

Alphas are Popular

I am not saying that popularity contests are important, but the fact is that alphas are well-liked and respected by those around them. While they can be intimidating to those who are not used to them, alpha males and females have a magnetic personality that draws people in like a magnet. While there will be plenty of people hoping you fail, you will also have your own cheering squad to keep you motivated. Either way, your mental toughness will make you a winner, whether people like you or not.

Amazing Leadership Skills

Think about the best leaders you have met and think about the traits they possessed. I am willing to bet they were more alpha than anything else. This is because alpha style personalities make the best leaders whether they are assigned an official role or not. People naturally want to follow alphas. They will respect your work and the way you carry yourself. The interesting thing is, if you work within an organization and aren't given an official leadership role, you will still be looked upon as the boss because of your unique characteristics. If you make a plan, others will abide by it.

Great at Problem-Solving
Alphas are great at coming up with solutions to various problems. This is because they are proactive and ready to come up with a plan. After this, they are ready to execute it.

Have Confidence, Charm, and Charisma
You are great at inspiring others, and people will glean from you because of how you make them feel. Your overall demeanor is very attractive to people because you are warm and welcoming. A lot of people believe that alphas are standoffish. They can sense fake people from a distance, but those whom they trust will be treated well.

Having a Can-Do attitude
Alphas get things done because they believe they can. Phrases like, "that's too hard," or "I can't do that," will not exist in their vocabulary. Whenever a task or challenge comes up, you will be ready to tackle it. Also, you will complete it with poise and grace as your feathers will not be ruffled. Even the most difficult projects will be no match for you.

Being Highly Ambitious
You have big plans for your life and are ready to make things happen. You do not think on a small scale as you want to reach heights no one else ever imagined for you. Alphas are never satisfied living a normal life. They want to do more every day.

Being Competitive
Life is a competition, and there is no way around it. If you want the best things in life, you will have to prove that you're more deserving of them than the thousands of other people going after the same goals. If you want to get a job, so do many other applicants. If you want to go to college, so do many other students. As an alpha, you will be ready to compete with the drive you have.

Controlling Your Own Life
An alpha will always control his or her destiny, and they know this. The victim mentality will never enter their thoughts because they know they are responsible for how their life turns out. If someone is trying to disrupt their pursuits, they will immediately be extricated from the alpha's life. These personality types have no time for that drama.

These are just some of the reasons why alphas are successful in their paths, whether it is a career, health, or personal relationships. If you are ready to start becoming an alpha, then it's time to go back and reread the strategies on mental toughness and also incorporate some of the action steps in the next section.

Cultivate Your Alpha Personality

These action steps are geared toward becoming an alpha. I advise you to work on these strategies, along with the many action steps from chapter four. Becoming an alpha is a lifelong process, which means you will always be improving and learning. The day you stop improving, you stop growing, and your life essentially comes to a halt. An alpha realizes that the only thing standing in the way of their dreams are themselves. This is why they get out of their own way. If you want to start cultivating the alpha mindset of fearlessness and toughness, then start performing the following strategies.

- Create a clear vision in your mind about the future you wish to have. Professionals from all backgrounds use this method to gain what they want in life. Before an athlete wins a big game, he or she visualizes themselves doing so. Don't just visualize the end result, but also how you plan to get there. It may not be perfect, but you will have a blueprint in your mind.
- Your body language shapes who you are and conveys it to the rest of the world. Walking around with your shoulders hunched forward and your head down is a subordinate position and will give you the same attitude. Therefore, paying attention to your posture is extremely important. When you walk confidently with your shoulders back, and your head held high, you will convey positivity and feel the same way on the inside.
- Don't just step outside of your comfort zone, but learn to live outside of it permanently. As a result, you will be faced with more obstacles and be forced to come up with more solutions. You will fall down much more often, but the result you obtain will be much greater.
- Start leading in your own life. If you follow the first three steps, then people are more likely to believe in you, and therefore, follow you. People love to follow those with a vision, show confidence, and have the guts to make things happen.
- Stop saying the word "no." So, this one might be a little confusing since I have been urging you to say "no." However, context is important here. You must stop saying "no" when it comes to opportunities and start pursuing things with grit. It will open up more possibilities for you.
- Learn to smile more. People have a tendency to mirror the emotions of those whom they are with. If you are one to smile a lot, then others will like you more. This will make you more influential.
- Stop playing bystander and start taking action. The bystander effect is when people simply stand around because they think someone else will handle the situation. The alphas are the ones

who jump in first and get the job done. Stop being a bystander and start becoming an alpha.
- Dress to impress and showcase your personality. Alphas care about their appearance because it is a representation of their personality. Alphas are known to be strong and confident, which is showcased by the clothes they wear.
- Start changing your inner circle. If you want to become a mentally tough alpha, then you need to be around others who are the same way.

"You are the average of the five people you spend the most time with."
-Jim Rohn

The Misconceptions About an Alpha

Unfortunately, alphas do not have the best reputation in today's world. At a time when aggression is looked down upon, their strong personalities stand out and do not go over well for many people. Alpha males are looked at as toxic, while alpha females are looked at as bossy or power-hungry. This is a bad sign because being an alpha is a good thing, and the world would benefit greatly if there were more of them. With the personality traits and benefits that come from them, it is a wonder why alphas are not more revered in our society. A major reason is because of the misconceptions that people have.

Alphas are associated with many negative traits, but these are assigned unfairly to these individuals. Being a true alpha is not about having the negative attributes that so many people think of. Alphas are strong people who bring so much value to everyone, and it's time we learn the truth about who they are. The following are some common misconceptions of the alpha that many people believe. I will break these down based on gender because society thinks differently between men and women.

Alpha Males

Alpha males are generally the leaders of any pack, both humans and animals included. The term toxic masculinity has become common to describe men who display negative attributes. Men have become degraded by so many people, including other men, so any type of aggression is seen as threatening. The term toxic masculinity is often used towards men who display alpha qualities; however, alphas don't actually behave in this perceived manner. Here are some common falsities associated with alpha males.
- They are not abusive, domineering, or trying to be bullies. This is quite the opposite. Alphas have a high confidence level, so they don't need to dominate or bully others to make themselves feel

good. Sometimes, their strong personalities can be off putting to people, but their goal is to get things done and not put others down. In fact, an alpha male will go out of his way to encourage and praise someone.
- They are not rude or arrogant. Once again, their confidence gets misinterpreted for arrogance. The alpha male does not think he is better than anyone else, but he will work hard to create the best life for himself.
- He is not self-serving and selfish. The alpha male does believe in self-care. He will take care of his needs before anyone else's and expects other people to do the same for themselves.
- Alpha males are not uncaring or uncompassionate. They highly care about other people and have compassion, but they also respect honesty. An alpha male will be honest way before he is nice. However, he is not this way to be mean, but to be helpful.
- Alpha males do not think less of women. In fact, they will encourage and even help a woman succeed in their lives because they are not threatened by it. Real men, like alphas, are not terrified of strong women.
- They will not use you and then throw you to the side. If an alpha male asks for help in the first place, that means he really needs it. He will always appreciate the help and pay it back or pay it forward in the long run.
- They enjoy having fun; however, they know when it's time for work and when it's time for play and don't mix the two up.
- An alpha male knows how to express himself. He does not bottle up his emotions, but actually expresses them in a healthy manner. This includes knowing the time and place to let them out.

Alpha males possess the good qualities of being a man. Essentially, toxic masculinity is an oxymoron because true masculinity is not toxic. A real man who is mentally tough knows how to treat himself and others.

Alpha Females

There has been a surge of strong females in our society over the past few decades, which is a good thing. Of course, there have always been strong women throughout history, but they were not always allowed to show their toughness. They were often expected to be low-key, agreeable, and supportive. They were kept down by society and even seen as lower-class individuals. With the emergence of the alpha female, more women have been able to express themselves and hold positions that were once dominated by men.

Unfortunately, this emergence has also led to many misconceptions about what an alpha female is. They are mentally tough people who strive to win in life. In many cases, women have to be mentally tougher than men because they are viewed in a more negative light if they show

strength. They get many different insults thrown at them, and what makes things worse is that many of them come from other women. The following are some of the misconceptions related to alpha females.
- They are not mean or rude. Alpha females have no problem being sarcastic and will expect you to give it back to them. Some people take this as being rude when, in reality, they are just having fun being playful. If an alpha female does not like you, she probably won't talk to you. Her sarcasm is a way of opening up.
- They are not the "B" word. Alpha females have a backbone and are not afraid to stand up or themselves. If you think they will be submissive, you have got another thing coming. They are not doing this to look bad, but they realize if they don't stand up for themselves, they will get walked all over.
- They are not drama queens. People take an alpha female's bluntness for wanting to create drama. The reason they are blunt is to avoid drama at all costs. They despise it and don't want anything to do with it. An alpha female would rather get work done than deal with other people's issues. As a result, they don't like to waste time arguing and just want to get to the point.
- Alpha females are not high maintenance; They just know what they want and expect to get it. If you have an alpha female as a girlfriend or a wife, she will be very loving, but not a doormat. If you try to walk on her, you will probably end up tripping badly.
- Alpha females are not insensitive, but they may not get gooey and emotional like other women. Her hard exterior is a way to deal with the world, and underneath, it might be the most sensitive person you will ever meet.
- Alpha females do not think they're right all the time. They will certainly have opinions and beliefs that they'll standby, but they won't automatically shut off everything else. While they will challenge opinions, they will listen to them at the same time.
- Alpha females are not control-freaks. They will often take control of a situation because they have the confidence to do so, but they will never stick their nose where it doesn't belong.

Just like the alpha male, an alpha female becomes the leader of almost any group she is in. She is independent in her life and does not expect anyone to run it for her. If someone tries to control her, it won't end well for them.

The bottom line is, the more mentally tough you become and the better you are at mastering your emotions, the more alpha qualities you will possess. You will live your life the way you choose, and no one can tell you any different. Alphas are strong individuals, and we need them in our life.

Betas and Gammas

To get a full understanding of the alpha males and females, I will discuss their counterparts, betas, and Gammas. The ironic part is, the negative qualities that these personalities have are often associated with alphas.

Beta Personality

Betas are completely different personality types than alphas. They have more of the "nice person" reputation and are not known for being aggressive or challenging. Betas are more likely to go with the flow and avoid rocking the boat.

In regards to men, a beta male is more sensitive and easygoing. They are reliable but are not usually the leaders of a pack. They are more like followers, and just like to keep things easy. They have the "nice guy" persona all the way, which does have its setbacks. They often get overlooked for certain opportunities because they do not put themselves at the forefront. This includes being passed over for dates by girls they find attractive. Beta males are also more self-conscious about everything and often avoid risks because they are worried about getting embarrassed.

Beta males like to keep to themselves and avoid causing any disturbances. While alphas would never go along to get along, that is part of the beta's motto. A beta will work hard, have friends, and be very likable, but he won't be the most memorable person in any situation. When he's with a woman, he is terrified of saying the wrong thing, so he holds things in. When he's with his male friends, he will be afraid of getting exposed for being weak.

Beta males do make good romantic partners. In fact, many women choose this type of man because he is reliable and husband material. He will need to learn how to stand up for himself, especially if he's with a strong female.

In regards to beta females, they are good women like alpha females but don't get nearly the same amount of attention. This is because they are more likely to go with the flow and not challenge things. They often suffer in silence because they are afraid to express their true emotions. Even though she deserves good things in life, she gets overlooked because of not being forceful enough.

Beta females make great friends as they are ready to support anybody. She will prevent fights from happening because she won't upset anyone. These types of women will bend over backward to help people and completely ignore their own needs. This is because they believe no one will like them otherwise. While an alpha female couldn't care less if people like her, the beta female makes it her mission in life.

In the business world, the alpha and beta females will always go the extra mile, but for totally different reasons. The alpha wants to take charge and expand her career, while the beta just wants to please someone. In the end, a beta female deserves respect because she has earned what she has through hard work and effort.

Gamma Personality

I will now introduce the omega personality, which is the opposite of an alpha. They are usually known for their lack of courage and ability to stand up for themselves. In regards to males, gammas are quite shy and will never make the first move, whether it comes to career or asking a girl out. He has no interest in going the extra mile and just does the minimum to get the job completed.

Alphas and to a lesser degree, betas are usually the top of the food chain, gammas are just looking to survive and stay under the radar. These types of men simply nod along and never interject with anything. While the beta male will never rock the boat, the gamma will try to avoid it altogether.

As far as relationships go, gamma males are an extremely needy type. They will be obsessed with the women they like, and if they do end up dating someone, they will never let her off their sites. This can lead some gammas to becoming overly protective and even stalkers.

Gamma males have no self-esteem and, deep down, hate who they are. They want to change but have no idea how to. Finally, gamma males are the most openly sensitive types and will sympathize with people incessantly.

In regards to females, a gamma is also the complete opposite of an alpha. She likes to be caught by a man and wants a strong male presence in her life. However, she is not obsessed with finding a partner and will hold out for someone who really catches her eye. She is also more cooperative and will just go along with everyone else. Unlike the alpha, she is not happy to rock the boat, although she does feel comfortable in her skin.

As you can see, the personality types are all vastly different, and a lot of it has to do with how well they manage their emotions. As you learn to master your emotions, I hope you start reaping the benefits of being a powerful alpha.

CHAPTER 7
Being Mentally Tough In The Real World

I hope you have enjoyed reading about controlling your emotions and becoming more mentally tough. While I would love for the world to be a fun and easy place to live, that is not reality. Life can be tough, and you will be in situations that will challenge you regularly. Those who retreat become failures, while those who overcome rise to the top. For continued success in any situation, you must be mentally tough, and the strategies in the previous chapters are meant to help you become this way.

Now that I have provided you all the necessary information, the focus of this chapter will be to present real-life scenarios to showcase the value of mental toughness and emotional strength. I will present several cases and illustrate how a mentally tough, versus a mentally weak person would handle the situation.

James' Story

Version One:

James was going into work one morning. When he arrived, he was inundated with many different issues all at once. The place was literally falling apart because of employees quitting or acting. As a result, there were multiple deadlines that were missed. James' boss looked like he was having a nervous breakdown over the whole situation.

When he walked to his desk, James immediately got to work on the tasks that needed to be completed. There were many people either complaining or freaking out around him, but he completely ignored the noise. Instead, he remained focused on the projects, starting with the most urgent ones first. After this, he continued to complete various tasks based on importance and would help put out certain fires if they came his way.

About halfway through the day, James was starting to get stressed out, so he excused himself from his desk. He stepped outside for a few minutes and took some deep breaths. Afterward, he came back inside and got back to work immediately. He blocked his time to work on each project for 15-20 minutes at a time. He did not have time to make things perfect, but he made sure everything was acceptable. This served him pretty well.

James' coworkers noticed how efficiently he was getting things done, and decided to stop whining in order to get to work, as well. Together, they all completed numerous tasks and were able to get things organized. It was a long and busy day, but everything turned out much better than before.

By the end, the projects that were overdue and many of the ones that were due soon got completed. Because James' showed a lot of calmness and did not allow himself to get rattled, he was able to pay attention to the job at hand. In addition, his coworkers gleaned from his attitude and started mirroring his work ethic. Even though James was not a manager or higher-up, he was still seen as a leader because of his attitude and demeanor.

Before James showed up, everything was a mess, and it could be because James' boss was an emotional wreck. People were absorbing his feelings. After James showed up, the mood started to change. When a person acts mentally tough, he inspires others to act the same, just as James did.

Version Two:

James came into work and was immediately inundated with all of the problems going on. The place was literally falling apart as employees had quit or started acting up. James became completely overwhelmed and went to go sit at his desk. While trying to figure things out, he kept getting distracted by all of the noise around him. His boss was even having a nervous breakdown in his office.

James had piles of papers on his desk from projects that needed to be completed but did not know where to start. He was trying to read through the papers but kept getting distracted by so many things. The environment was getting louder and more disorganized by the minute.

About halfway through the day, James realized he did not get any work done, which sent him into a panic attack. Instead of stepping away for a few minutes, he hustled to try and get things finished. He even skipped lunch, which made him feel even worse.

By the end of the day, James barely got anything completed, his coworkers were still acting up, and his boss was nowhere to be found. On top of this, the workload piled up even more, which meant the following day would be even worse.

When James left for the day, he immediately went home and crashed in front of the TV, hoping to ignore the day altogether. As we watched some movies, he was still having anxiety from earlier in the day and could not seem to settle down. When he tried to sleep at night, he was too nervous thinking about the next day to be able to relax.

In version two of the story, James was not able to control his emotions, which negatively affected his workday. He was not able to help his workers relax, and everybody fed off each other's tension. Even though James was not to blame for the whole situation, he was not able to make it any better because he did not display any emotional control or mental toughness. As a result, he fell apart, and so did most of his coworkers.

Jill's Story

Version One:

Jill was driving her car on the freeway in heavy traffic. While she had to get somewhere on time, and even left early, the traffic was even worse than expected due to an accident. As a result, she would not arrive at her location on time. People were constantly cutting her off, and this did not make the situation better. However, Jill took several deep breaths and just kept driving, knowing she could not control the freeway and other cars.

As Jill was getting closer to her appointment time, she made a quick phone call to the person she was meeting to let her know she would be late. After this, she continued to drive with the flow of traffic. The times she could feel herself getting stressed, she would take a few deep breaths and start to feel better. Lucky for her, she also kept water in her car.

Jill eventually arrived at her appointment 30 minutes late, but since she was able to call early, the person was expecting it. Jill was also thankful she arrived safely because there were several accidents along the way, including some she watched in real-time.

Even though Jill was in a situation that would stress most people out and even make them angry, she was able to maintain her calmness. The last place you want to lose your cool is on a busy freeway.

Version Two:

Jill was running late to her appointment because she got stuck on the freeway in heavy traffic. It was even worse than she expected due to an accident. As she was driving, she became very frustrated with the lack of movement and quickly took an exit. Unfortunately, the traffic here was just as bad, if not worse. As a result, Jill had to find a way to get back on the freeway.

As she was going along, her anger continued to grow, and she kept trying to drive around people. This was not making her journey any quicker and only making things more dangerous. At one point, Jill almost collided with another car, which sent her into a cursing rage. She was already late for her meeting, but Jill did not think about calling ahead and letting the other person know. She was too worked up with the traffic situation that nothing else came to mind.

Ultimately, she arrived at her appointment almost an hour late, and the person she was meeting was not happy. She would have appreciated a phone call ahead of time. Jill was not interested in hearing about her frustrations. All she was concerned about was her stressful drive. The meeting was a disaster as both parties were not interested in hearing each other out. Basically, Jill wasted both of their time due to losing control of her emotions.

Jill's story in version two showcases how mastering your emotions and the art of mental toughness is imperative no matter what situation you are in.

Mike's Story

Version One:
Mike was working in his garage when he smelled smoke coming from inside the house. No one was home, so this was very unusual. When Mike went inside, he realized that the dishwasher blew a circuit, and a small fire was started. There was quite a bit of smoke coming out.

Mike became nervous, but took a deep breath and jumped into action. He remembered that there was a fire extinguisher upstairs, so he ran up real quick and got it. He pulled out the pin and swept the fire with the extinguisher, which put it out immediately. The dishwasher was partially damaged, but nothing else was touched. He could easily get a new dishwasher.

After this, Mike realized he needed more fire extinguishers, so he ran to the store to buy a few more. It would be helpful to have several located around the house for emergency purposes. Mike was able to remain calm and save his kitchen from being burned down.

Version Two:
Mike was working in his garage when he smelled some smoke coming from inside his house. It was odd because nobody was at home. Mike quickly ran in and bumped into a table along the way, which knocked everything over. When he looked into his kitchen, he noticed that the dishwasher blew a circuit and caught on fire.

Mike started panicking and began looking everywhere for a fire extinguisher. He began foraging through all of the cabinets in the kitchen, but could not find it anywhere. The fire was spreading beyond the dishwasher, which made Mike panic even more. After several minutes of searching everywhere, Mike decided to grab a pot and use it to pour water onto the fire. This created a lot of smoke in the house, but it was the only solution he could come up with.

Eventually, the fire went out, and the whole kitchen was filled with smoke. The cabinets and all of the appliances were covered in smoke dust. A few minutes after the fire ended, Mike remembered that the extinguisher was upstairs, which made him angrier.

If Mike would have kept his cool, he may have remembered where the fire extinguisher was. Instead, he wasted valuable minutes looking for it as the fire grew. Mental toughness and emotional control can truly help you in any situation you are in.

Tanya's Story

Version One:

Tanya was working out at the gym. She had already done 30 minutes on the treadmill and was now set to try the elliptical. Even though she was tired, she had to get ready for an upcoming event she would be involved with. After about five minutes on the new machine, Tanya was ready to give up. She wanted to do at least 15 more minutes, though. To get through, Tanya started taking some deep breaths and focused on the movement of her arms and legs. She did this for several minutes and realized she went another five minutes without even realizing it.

As Tanya continued to push forward, the minutes were passing, and she was getting closer to her goal. Eventually, the 15 minutes were up, and Tanya was not ready to stop. She decided to go another 10 minutes. As a result, Tanya got one of the best workouts of her life. If she had quit earlier, she would have been very disappointed, but because she kept going, there was something to be proud of.

Version Two:

Tanya went to the gym and began training on the treadmill. She was not feeling up to run anymore, so she quit after 10 minutes, which was half of her expected time. She wanted to go home at this point but decided to try out the elliptical. This workout came with the same results. Tany was just going through the motions and not really engaged in her training.

After about 10 minutes on the elliptical, Tanya was feeling tired and did not have the motivation to keep going. She could not allow herself to continue. She decided to get off the machine and call it a day. There was no real progress with the gym time, and Tanya felt like she wasted the trip. She had no desire to go back, though.

In Tanya's case, she was able to get motivation in the first version through mental toughness, but not in the second version, and you can see the outcomes of both scenarios.

I hope you enjoyed these scenarios, which showcase the power of mastering your emotions in many different settings.

CONCLUSION

Thank you for making it through to the end of *Mental Toughness*, let's hope it was informative and able to provide you with all of the tools you need to achieve your goals whatever they may be. We are taught so many things throughout our childhood and adult years, and a lot of it is centered around knowledge and skills. Society seems to be more concerned with how much a person knows than they are with how well they handle a situation. While knowledge is important, it is ultimately useless if it cannot be used in a practical manner. In order for this to occur, a person must be able to master their emotions.

The idea of emotional mastery relates to knowing and understanding our emotions at any given time and releasing them in a healthy and productive manner. Having various thoughts and feelings is normal; however, not managing them appropriately can lead to many poor outcomes, no matter what the situation is. Life is full of surprises, and events won't always go our way. We can be prepared and properly trained, but what matters most is how we react in real-time. When a person is faced with a challenging situation in a setting that is not in their favor, having control over their emotions is what will create the best outcomes. Essentially, laughing, being happy, getting angry, and becoming sad all have a time and a place. When you master your emotions, you will know exactly what that time and place are at every juncture.

Emotional mastery is related to the art of mental toughness, which is the ability to manage and overcome any doubts, worries, concerns, or circumstances that prevent you from succeeding. When you are mentally tough, life might bring you down, but it will never keep you down. This is because you have the fortitude to rise to the occasion, despite what the challenges might be. Mental toughness was a major discussion point in this book because of how important it is to achieve absolute success in life. In the end, it is not about what you know but how much you can handle in the face of adversity.

With each chapter, I explained in-depth the various topics associated with mastering your emotions and mental toughness and listed various exercises to help build these traits in your life. The strategies I went over are simple to understand but can be difficult to execute as they require a lot of effort and persistence. They are something that must become a lifestyle, so doing them on a regular basis is essential. I also went over the numerous benefits of being mentally tough, including the idea of becoming an alpha in your life. Once you become an alpha, you will be a winner in every aspect.

Unfortunately, mental toughness is lacking in our society, and it has not been given the attention it deserves. With this book, I hope to change that. My goal is to inspire other people to develop a strong mindset, so they have the capability to succeed in every facet of their lives. In the end, the qualities that sprout from mental toughness are what matter the most. It's what gets you through the toughest moments people find themselves in.

The next step is to take the information from this book and start incorporating it into your everyday routine. Knowledge without execution is ultimately worthless. Take every strategy and action step that I went over and start practicing them daily. Before you know it, they will become habits, and being mentally tough will be part of your nature. You will thank yourself in the end when you have life's challenges are no longer a stopping point, but a learning opportunity.

Finally, if you found this book useful in any way, a review on Amazon is always appreciated! I want as many individuals as possible to gain help from this book, and the more reviews it gets, the more people will know about it.

DESCRIPTION

How many different emotions do you feel throughout the day? If you are like everyone else, the answer is too many to count. Emotions are running through our minds at a rapid pace, and we have no real ability to shut them out. They are flowing endlessly, and our minds can become overwhelmed with so much chatter that we completely lose our mental clarity. Our thoughts and feelings make up who we are and lead to many of the decisions we make on a daily basis. Therefore, what we feel determines our life's outcomes. If we cannot organize our thoughts and feelings, then our actions also become erratic.

Another question to ask is, do you have an immediate reaction to your emotions? For those of you who said yes, I can help you with this situation. The Idea of mastering your emotions is not blocking, suppressing, or ignoring them. On the contrary, it means recognizing they exist, assessing what they mean, and managing them, so they are used for our benefit. Emotions are not inherently good or bad. There is a time and a place for all of them. What we do with these emotions determines good or evil.

When we achieve emotional mastery, the world becomes our oyster. We obtain the ability to overcome any obstacles thrown at us, perform at our highest levels even during the most challenging times, and will achieve the goals we set out for. While there is no measurement of emotional mastery or intelligence, it is considered by many to be more important than intelligence or skill level. If you can't master your emotions, then all of your other attributes won't matter in the long run.

The foundation of all of this is mental toughness, which means you have the ability to succeed over the highest levels of adversity. Mental toughness is not something you're born with, but something you develop through your environment, or with specific action steps that target your mindset. Throughout the chapters in this book, I will cover:

- The idea of mastering your emotions and what it means to your life.
- The importance of emotional intelligence and controlling your situation.
- What mental toughness is, the benefits it creates, and the many strategies you can use to develop it within yourself.
- What having a strong mindset looks like.
- How having mental toughness can lead you to become an alpha.
- The success that comes from an alpha mindset.
- Hypothetical situations that illustrate how mental toughness works in real-life situations.

Mental toughness and emotional mastery are not optional characteristics to have if you want to succeed consistently in your life. It does not matter if it's with your career, personal relationships, or health; having a strong mindset means the difference between winners and losers, as well as happiness and misery. Lucky for us, all of this can be learned, which is the objective of this book.

If you are ready to stop being a victim and take full control of your life, then it's time to take action. Start reading this book and using the knowledge to change your life and circumstances. It all starts with the mind, so build up your mental toughness now and start living the life you want. Waiting any longer only delays achieving your desired goals.

www.ingramcontent.com/pod-product-compliance
Lightning Source LLC
Chambersburg PA
CBHW071452070526
44578CB00001B/322